MEDITATION IN FLOWERS

ACKNOWLEDGEMENTS

TO

The original occasion which prompted the idea of holding a
'Meditation in Flowers' as a Church Flower Festival . . .

The Ninth Centenary Year of
the foundation of the Parish
Church at Milborne St. Andrew
in Dorset

AND TO

The Dorset Floral Decoration Society

whose members co-operated in
every detail to make the Flower
Festival and this small book
possible

AND TO

My brother-in-law, John Harding

for the photographs in the
illustrated editions

The Parish Church,
Milborne Saint Andrew, Dorset.

ARRANGEMENTS 19 AND 20—EASTER (The Gate of Everlasting Life)

The East window (1885) was given in memory of Roger Gresley (Vicar: 1878-79) by his son Nigel (Vicar: 1879-87). CARDINAL MORTON was born in Milborne St. Andrew, as also was the father of GEORGE ORWELL, Richard Blair. Richard's father was Vicar 1854-67.

MEDITATION IN FLOWERS

A FLOWER FESTIVAL GUIDE
(without illustrations)
OR
A BOOK FOR THE BEDSIDE TABLE
(with illustrations)

DESIGNED FOR PRIVATE
MEDITATION ON THEMES
OF THE CHURCH'S YEAR

BY THE REV.
JOHN L. BAILLIE, A.K.C.

'We also should walk in newness of life'

Romans vi.4

CLARIUS·PUBLICATIONS

First published
without illustrations

JUNE 1967

with illustrations
DECEMBER 1967

by

CLARIUS PUBLICATIONS

THE VICARAGE
MILBORNE ST. ANDREW
BLANDFORD FORUM
DORSET

Binding by

PITMAN PRESS
Bath

BAYNTUN
Bath

Colour reproduction by
BAILEY AND WELLMAN LTD
Church Lane, Clifton Wood Road, Bristol.

Colour printing by
GILDEN PRINT
Fishponds, Bristol.

Letterpress printing by
FRIARY PRESS
Longmans (Dorchester Ltd.) Dorset.

FLOWERS AT THE FEET OF JESUS

A hymn for any Flower Festival   (Tune: A. & M. 115).

Flowers at the feet of JESUS
Before Thine altar stay,
Those blessed hours Thou giv'st us
In which we kneel and pray.

Those flowers in meet obeisance
Which nestle at Thy feet;
Keep us from all complaisance
More fearful Thou to greet.

Those dear, sweet, upturned faces
So pure, so calm, so fair,
Which rest in Holy places
And look so lovely there.

So turn we then to JESUS
And worship at His feet;
Who knows us as He sees us
More worthy Him to meet.

MARY WEBB

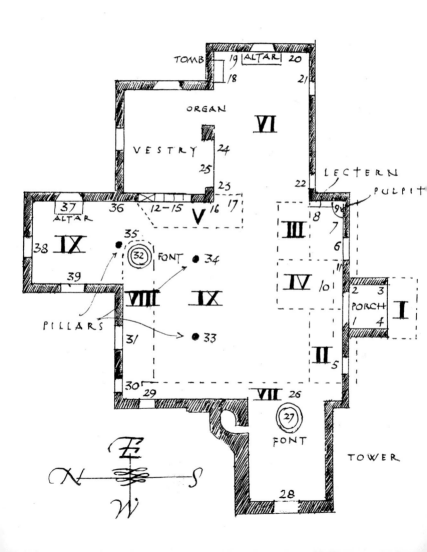

GROUND PLAN
ST·ANDREW'S CHURCH
MILBORNE ST ANDREW – DORSET

TOMB   19 | ALTAR | 20
18   21

ORGAN   VI

VESTRY   24
25
23
37   36   12–15   16 17
ALTAR   V
35
38 IX   ●32 FONT ●34
39
VIII   IX
PILLARS
31   ●33
30
29

37
ALTAR

LECTERN
PULPIT
22
III   8
7
6
IV   10   11
2   3
PORCH I
1   4

II   5

VII   26
27
FONT

TOWER
28

E
N   S
W

CONTENTS

LIST OF COLOUR ILLUSTRATIONS & ARRANGERS

PREFACE

In thirty years of adult life, I have spent about a third of my time involved in Army Communications of one sort or another during service in the Royal Signals. Even during so short a time as a decade the methods and equipment changed several times, but the messages sent were much the same. When secret they became more secure, and when not so, they became more vocal and deserted the drudgery of the morse code. I have spent the other two-thirds of my time as an ordained Priest of the Church of England, involved in the Church's communications between God and Man, and between Man and God. In all this time the messages I have had to receive and pass either way have been much the same, and likewise the message I have to give about my Saviour is very much the same as it always has been, except perhaps in that I know Him now more intimately through long association. But I am sure that the Ministers of the Church, not excepting myself, are far too slow to seek out and use new means of communication. Perhaps we are afraid of new methods and equipment lest they should appear to degrade the divine message, and therefore we prefer the safety of such accustomed usage as the Victorian or Jacobean pulpit.

This book is concerned with only one small attempt, in an equally small village, to find a new method of communicating Christian Truths. I see the possibility of floral arrangements (mundane things in themselves, but so are bread and wine) as a modern means of drawing more attention to the Church's Year, and thereby communicating Christian teaching. In many different circumstances of life, it is an accepted custom throughout the world, that gifts of flowers are used as expressions of different emotions where words would be inadequate. We all try to communicate with people through flowers in this way. Equally we are accustomed to use flowers to express the general theme of beauty, or to enhance the beauty of people or things.

The greater part of 'Meditation in Flowers' is concerned with nine great themes of the Church's Year depicted in floral arrangements for a particular Flower Festival.

The text for each theme is divided into three sections: the first has appropriate 'Readings' from the New English Bible translation of the liturgical Epistles and Gospels; the second has 'Meditations' on the 'Readings' and the Collects for the day; the third is a confession of personal faith in the lordship of Jesus, which presents a continuous message throughout the book and occasionally describes in greater detail the meaning of the flower arrangement pictures in relation to this message.

Chapter X of the book has been added in response to a request made by many who read the booklet published without illustrations at the time of the festival.

Space would not allow a comprehensive study of the many possibilities in this new approach, but I thought that a few 'briefings' for Church Flower Festivals might be helpful towards the stimulation of ideas for the correlation of flower festivals with Christian teaching. For this, pre-planning and an overall pattern for the occasion are essentials. But it is not suggested that the 'briefings' set out in this chapter should be slavishly carried out.

It seems to me that if a Minister decides to have a flower festival in a Church, he must do more than engage a Floral Decoration Society to do it and leave every detail to them. I am sure that I am right in saying that any Society will appreciate the guidance of the Minister in everything in which he is an authority, such as the themes to be portrayed and the overall pattern for the occasion. And this does not just consist of giving the festival a name for use on the advertising posters. It means a good deal of thought and planning, and after that, liaison and guidance. And a wise Minister will accept the authority of the F.D.S. as to the correct mechanics of flower arranging. Many things can be done in this art, which might seem impossible to him, and there are many things which might seem appropriate to him but quite unsuitable to the arranger.

When it is considered that many parishioners and visitors (in our case 1,700 in the heart of the country) will attend the festival, it is surely an obligation upon the Minister to contribute some message of the Church's teaching through so instructive a visual aid.

Once he has briefed the F.D.S. as to the theme in some such detail as I have suggested in Chapter X, it is equally important that he leaves them quite free as to how they depict his briefing both collectively and individually by floral arrangement. For they are the experts in this and can be relied upon to produce excellent results, and ask for the Minister's advice if they need it.

When all was in place for our festival I made a personal tour around all the arrangements and studied them carefully. It was an exciting experience to find that despite all I had tried to contribute to the occasion and all I had written for the 'Meditations', my own personal understanding of the themes depicted was deepened and enlarged by the artistry of the arrangers and the supervisory skill of Mrs. Cara Barne. Some of this understanding I have tried to pass on to the reader in my passages on the lordship of Jesus.

My aim in this book is to suggest that all Church flower festivals become more useful and instructive if a companion manual is produced of either meditations, teachings, devotions or such like related to the themes depicted in the floral arrangements.

The holding of Flower Festivals in Churches has become a popular activity in comparatively recent times. And such Festivals have been proved as successful fund-raisers. Large crowds are attracted to them for the two to four days of their duration. But ought we to be satisfied with the welcome revenue they bring? Ought we not also to use them as occasions for the proclamation of the Gospel? What message from God's Church do the weekday visitors to a Flower Festival take home with them? It is true that there is the beauty of His creation in the flowers, or an atmosphere of reverence in the Church, but what of the urgent messages of the Church's Faith?

It is my hope that through this 'Meditation in Flowers', as an occasion and as a book, some at least of these messages shall be written.

To-day in some way or another members of the Church are compelled to meditate upon the questions put to their faith, either by the so-called New Theology, or by the environment of a humanistic populace, less and less of whom witness to a faith in Christ by acts of public worship. The questions which compel us to stop and to meditate might run on in such verses as these:

WHAT CAN I NOW BELIEVE?

i

And where have all our doctrines gone?
  What can I now believe?
Let's 'follow-me-leader', and throw
  them away!
  There is no settled belief!

ii

And where has the Fast of Advent gone?
  What can I now believe?
Let's 'follow-me-leader', and live-it-up
  more!
  There is no need to repent!

iii

And where has the Birth by Virgin gone?
  What can I now believe?
Let's 'follow-me-leader', and find a new
  creed
  So that there is no offence!

iv

And where has the Star of Epiphany gone?
  What can I now believe?
Let's 'follow-me-leader' or a cosmonaut
  And search throughout the heavens!

v

But some still keep the Lenten Fast;
  What meaneth this belief?
A suffering world is with us yet,
  This truth is clear to see!

vi

And on Good Friday some keep watch;
  What meaneth this belief?
A suffering world yet has the hope
  That He may set it free!

vii

But where is the Hope of Easter?
  What can I now believe?
Did He, or didn't He rise from the dead?
  Give me an answer! Give!

viii

And where has the Ascended gone?
  What can I now believe?
Let's follow-me-leader, avoiding the
  stairs
  Jacob and Jesus knew!

ix

And where's the Holy Spirit gone?
  What can I now believe?
Let's 'follow-me-leader', and look deep
  down,
  For, 'THOU SHALT NOT LOOK UP!'

x

And where's the Holy Trinity gone?
  What can I now believe?
Let's 'follow-me-leader', and leave this
  one out,
  The Mystery's too great!

In our small but eleventh century village Church at Milborne Saint Andrew in Dorset, we are carrying out a restoration of its fabric and, using the Church's Year as our guide, we are seeking to extend this restoration to our faith as well.

We seek an answer to the question: 'What can I now believe?' In our Flower Festival, as this little book will show, I have kept to the same theme, but I have brought most of the Year into one great occasion. And I hope that the reader will be led to confess, confirm, restore, or strengthen his or her faith in 'Jesus as Lord'.

Finally, and in the meaning of the Collect for Easter Day—I pray humbly that as by God's special grace He puts into our minds good desires, so by His continual help we may bring the same to good effect.

NEW TESTAMENT REFERENCES

REFERENCES TO THE NEW TESTAMENT ARE TAKEN FROM THE NEW ENGLISH BIBLE, NEW TESTAMENT © 1961 OXFORD AND CAMBRIDGE UNIVERSITY PRESSES. WHERE THE REFERENCE IS PART OF THE SET EPISTLE OR GOSPEL FOR A SUNDAY OR RED LETTER DAY ACCORDING TO THE BOOK OF COMMON PRAYER, THIS FACT IS STATED AND THE BOOK, CHAPTER, AND VERSES ARE NOT INDICATED. WHERE THE REFERENCE IS NOT A PART OF THE SET EPISTLE OR GOSPEL, THE BOOK, CHAPTERS AND VERSES ARE INDICATED.

Chapter I

•

ST. ANDREW

MISSION

•

READINGS FROM THE EPISTLE FOR ST. ANDREW'S DAY

MEDITATION ON THE EPISTLE FOR ST. ANDREW'S DAY

•

ARRANGEMENTS 1-4

1 & 2   Reaching out into the world

3 & 4   Drawing into the Church

•

Jesus is Lord

ARRANGEMENT 1   REACHING OUT INTO THE WORLD   ARRANGEMENT

The porch of a Church is an appropriate position in which to place two or mor arrangements depicting missionary activity and St. Andrew's Day.

ARRANGEMENT 3   DRAWING INTO THE CHURCH   ARRANGEMENT 4

These two arrangements welcome the visitors and guide their eyes to the door of the Church with its Norman arch and outward reaching arrangements (1 and 2). Red—the liturgical colour for the Feast has been used throughout.

ARRANGEMENT 2   A FISHER OF MEN   ARRANGEMENT

A net has been hung between these two arrangements to associate the theme with
St. Andrew the fisherman. On the stone seat opposite (see Arrangement 1 overleaf) two
other accessories (a brass tray and a wooden boat—missionary exhibits from India) have
been used to emphasise the theme of mission.

I. ST. ANDREW—MISSION

Readings from the Epistle for St. Andrew's Day

CONFESSION, FAITH, AND SALVATION

If on your lips is the confession, 'Jesus is Lord', and in your heart the faith that God raised him from the dead, then you will find salvation.

THE CALL TO SPREAD THE NEWS

How could they have faith in one they had never heard of? And how hear without someone to spread the news? And how could anyone spread the news without a commission to do so?

THE UNIVERSAL NEED

Scripture affirms: 'How welcome are the feet of the messengers of good news . . . . Their voice has sounded all over the earth, and their words to the bounds of the inhabited world'.

AGAINST A BACKGROUND OF INDIFFERENCE

But not all have responded to the good news . . . . 'All day long I have stretched out my hands to an unruly and recalcitrant people'.

The Collect for Saint Andrew's Day

Almighty God, who didst give such grace unto thy holy Apostle Saint Andrew, that he readily obeyed the calling of thy Son Jesus Christ, and followed him without delay; Grant unto us all, that we, being called by thy holy Word, may forthwith give up ourselves obediently to fulfil thy holy commandments; through the same Jesus Christ our Lord. Amen.

Meditation on the Epistle for St. Andrew's Day

FOR CONFESSORS IN THEIR CALLING

Do I show in every part of my life that God has raised Jesus from the dead? And do I speak out my faith with my lips? And to which of my neighbours ought I to be sent with the news which is in my heart? And if I myself cannot go overseas, when did I last send help to God's messengers in distant parts of the world? And what missionary work do I do in the locality in which I live?

THE UNIVERSAL QUESTION FOR CONFESSORS

Do these questions disturb your peace of mind? If they do you are true to your confession and calling. Do you ask: 'How can I feel warm towards those who have not heard or who are indifferent? For I am often as indifferent to them as they are to God'.

AGAINST A BACKGROUND OF FAITH

There is only one remedy. Believe in your heart, more and more, that God has raised Jesus from the dead. Then your resolve will find the urgency it needs. This faith alters life and gives purpose to living. You *may* find it as you follow this Meditation in Flowers through the Church's Year. And you *will* find it when you open the door of the Church and approach the Altar. For *there* is the joy and the glory and the victory of living and 'Jesus is Lord'.

Jesus is Lord

Mission has been the sub-title of our Reading and Meditation for Saint Andrew's Day. Throughout there has been a persistent emphasis on the profession of faith that 'Jesus is Lord'. It will be found that aspects of this emphasis come to light in the remaining chapters.

For the believer, personal acceptance of the lordship of Jesus is a fundamental necessity, without which his discipleship would be vanity. And missionary activity itself will be false unless its purpose is the proclamation that 'Jesus is Lord' in every department of life and personal living.

As we study the floral arrangements depicting St. Andrew's Day and Mission, we see that the two either side of the early Norman porch reach from the church door out into the world. Does not this compel our minds to consider that it is the task of the members of the Church to take their knowledge of the lordship of Jesus out into the world? But 'to go out and not to bring in' should be of the same concern to us as it was to the fishermen who toiled all night and caught no fish. Their failure was turned to success when they took their lord and master with them. On arrival the first flowers we see point the way into the church in welcome, and as we leave to go out with our message they remind us of the need to return and to bring others with us. It should not be difficult for the reader to extend still further thoughts such as these in association with the net which hangs on the wall, or the missionary exhibits on the stone seat opposite.

We ought always to remember that in all things 'Jesus is Lord', and that whatever lordship is granted to us on earth becomes vanity and takes on an artificiality unless it obeys His laws and glorifies Him.

This being so, we will do well to elaborate on this theme. Even at the level of obedience to our earthly masters, our intention must not be that of currying favour with men, but out of reverence for the Lord (Col.iii.22).

"Whatever you are doing, put your whole heart into it, as if you were doing it for the Lord and not for men, knowing that there is a master who will give you your heritage as a reward for your service. Christ is the master whose slaves you must be." (Col.iii.23 and 24).

We have the words of Jesus himself to assure us on this point:

"Turning to the assembled Pharisees Jesus asked them, 'What is your opinion about the Messiah? Whose son is he?' 'The son of David', they replied. 'How then is it', he asked, 'that David by inspiration calls him "Lord"? For he says, "The Lord said unto my Lord, 'sit at my right hand until I put your enemies under your feet.'" If David calls him "Lord", how can he be David's son?" (Gospel, Trinity XVIII).

David was inspired to make this claim and so is the Christian, and St. Paul writes to impress upon the Corinthians that:

"No one who says 'a curse on Jesus!' can be speaking under the influence of the spirit of God. And no one can say, 'Jesus is Lord!' except under the influence of the Holy Spirit." (Epistle, Trinity X).

———

Any reader actively engaged in a parish for the encouragement of interest in Overseas Missions might do well to consider the possibilities of combining a Missionary Exhibition with a Flower Festival. It was hoped that a 'briefing' on such a Festival might have been included in Chapter X. But time did not permit the gathering of sufficient information about exhibits available, and the floral arrangements would need to be briefed by an expert in flower arranging after studying such exhibits. But it seems possible that an excursion into this field of activity would accomplish two ends. First, it would tax the ingenuity of flower arrangers in a new and exciting way and give them a new range of expression in which to work. And second, it would provide an opportunity for members of the public to see the many wonderful missionary exhibits in a new environment.

Another very interesting addition to such a Festival of Missionary Exhibition might be the use of flowers, foliage, or driftwood, etc., provided by particular Overseas Missions.

Chapter II

•

ADVENT

PREPARATION

•

READINGS FROM THE EPISTLES OR GOSPELS FOR ADVENT

MEDITATION ON THE EPISTLES AND GOSPELS FOR ADVENT

•

ARRANGEMENT 5

Darkness to Light

•

Make the Lord's highway straight

ARRANGEMENT 5—DARKNESS TO LIGHT

The liturgical colour for Advent, which is a penitential season, is VIOLET or BLU
Here hues of the appropriate colour are used to depict the 'Darkness to Light' theme
the season's teaching. Many churches have no floral decorations during penitent
seasons, but would this tradition be outraged if the arrangements adhered to the corre
liturgical colour? If not—then the Feasts of Saint Andrew (November 30th) and Sai
Thomas (December 21), both in Advent, could be used to introduce shades of RE
also expressing the theme 'Darkness to Light'.

II. ADVENT—PREPARATION

Readings from the Epistles or Gospels for Advent

FROM DARKNESS TO LIGHT

. . . the whole law is summed up in love. In all this, remember how critical the moment is. It is time for you to wake out of sleep, for deliverance is nearer to us now than it was when we first believed. It is far on in the night; day is near. Let us therefore throw off the deeds of darkness and put on our armour as soldiers of the light. (Epistle, Advent I)

AS THE DAY APPROACHES

. . . portents will appear in sun, moon, and stars. On earth nations will stand helpless, not knowing which way to turn from the roar and surge of the sea . . . and then they will see the Son of Man coming on a cloud with great power and glory. When all this begins to happen, stand upright and hold your heads high, because your liberation is near. (Gospel, Advent II)

THE REVELATION COMES

. . . pass no premature judgement; wait until the Lord comes. For he will bring to light what darkness hides. (Epistle, Advent III)

AFTER WARNING AND PREPARATION

. . . 'I am the voice of one crying in the wilderness, "Make the Lord's highway straight".' (Gospel, Advent IV)

The Collect for Advent Sunday

Almighty God, give us grace that we may cast away the works of darkness, and put upon us the armour of light, now in the time of this mortal life, in which thy Son Jesus Christ came to visit us in great humility; that in the last day, when he shall come again in his glorious Majesty to judge both the quick and the dead, we may rise to the life immortal, through him who liveth and reigneth with thee and the Holy Spirit, now and ever. Amen.

Meditation on the Epistles and Gospels for Advent

In every moment of the Birth, Life, Death, Resurrection, Ascension and Glory of Jesus we see how critical God's Love is towards us. Advent is a season of preparation for a critical moment of God's Love; whether it be by the remembrance of the Birth of the Redeemer, or by the expectation of the Coming Judgement in the full power and glory of the dazzling Light of the Ascended Christ. When we first believed our love was great, and yet deliverance is nearer to us now than it was then. 'Darkness to Light' is a topical theme of all life within and around us. In all our meditations there is a sense in which our understanding is reborn when a shaft of the Light of the Gospel Truth penetrates the darkness of our minds.

We prepare for Christmas as though Jesus might come to us again through the crib of Bethlehem. This remembrance brings some Light. But the Light we need most at Advent, we avoid. We grasp the Light of the past but avoid the Light of the future. Faced with the future we dodge back into darkness. The Gospel tells us to prepare for His Coming with great power and glory. Are we prepared for this kind of Advent? Do we want to be judged? Do we want to be liberated from the darkness of this world? Do we know how near our liberation is? And what have we done to help to make the Lord's highway straight? These are the Advent questions crying in the dark wilderness of our hearts.

Make the Lord's Highway Straight

What does this distant cry from the wilderness mean for the Christian today? Where is the Lord's highway and how can he help to make it straight? St. John the Baptist, was quoting a much earlier cry from the desert, and the full quotation may help to answer these questions:

"Comfort ye, comfort ye my people, saith your God. Speak ye comfortably to Jerusalem, and cry unto her, that her warfare is accomplished, that her iniquity is pardoned: for she hath received of the Lord's hand double for all her sins.

"The voice of him that crieth in the wilderness, Prepare ye the way of the Lord, make straight in the desert a highway for our God. Every valley shall be exalted, and every mountain and hill shall be made low: and the crooked shall be made straight, and the rough places plain: and the glory of the Lord shall be revealed, and all flesh shall see it together: for the mouth of the Lord hath spoken it. The voice said Cry. And he said, What shall I cry? All flesh is grass, and all the goodliness thereof is as the flower of the field: the grass withereth, the flower fadeth: because the spirit of the Lord bloweth upon it: surely the people is grass. The grass withereth, the flower fadeth: but the word of our God shall stand for ever." (Isaiah XL.1-8 (AV)).

From this it is clear that the ROAD WORKS AHEAD for the Christian is the proclamation of the gospel that when Jesus is accepted as Lord there is a promise of comfort, of the accomplishment of warefare, and of the pardoning of inquity. The way in which the Christian can help to make the Lord's highway straight must therefore depend upon his knowledge of the Word of the Lord in scripture, and his desire to make it known to others with whom he lives and works and speaks. All this he can do in the power of the Holy Spirit. For Jesus said:

" . . . when he comes who is the Spirit of truth, he will guide you into all the truth; for he will not speak on his own authority, but will tell only what he hears: and he will make known to you the things that are coming. He will glorify me, for everything that he makes known to you he will draw from what is mine . . . " (Gospel, Easter V).

Perhaps part of the ineffectiveness of the evangelistic impact of the Church's mission today is due to failure to emphasise the true Christian belief that Jesus is Lord of all. Not just of the Christian, but of all mankind, and of all creation is he truly God; and as perfect man he is the Word of God, the Way (or highway), the Truth, and the Life.

Unless a man or woman accept this he cannot be a Christian by profession of faith in any New Testament sense.

What then of the question: 'Where is the Lord's highway'?

In the days of Isaiah it was the desert, in the days of the Baptist and Jesus it was the roads out of town. For to be found there were the good and the bad, the Jew and the Gentile. It was the poor and the outcast, and the hopeless that were to be found in the highway. Again we see this in one of Jesus's parables:

" . . . Then he said to his servants, 'The wedding-feast is ready; but the guests I invited did not deserve the honour. Go out to the main thoroughfares, and invite everyone you can find to the wedding.' The servants went out into the streets, and collected all they could find, good and bad alike. So the hall was packed with guests.'' (Gospel, Trinity XX)

But where is the Lord's highway today? It is surely wheresoever those sons and daughters of God foregather who either have not heard the Word of Life, or could-not-care-less about it, or who find it too hard a road to travel because their understanding of it is darkened by the glittering attractions of an affluent and worldly society. Does all this help the Christian to answer these questions in his or her own life and action for Jesus as Lord? The answer must rest with each individual's interpretation of the needs of the people he can reach with the joy and glory of living which is in his heart through Christ Jesus.

For a summary of our Advent preparation whether we look back down the highway to the birth of Jesus at Bethlehem, or forward and out along the highway to His coming in majesty and glory when all men and all creation shall bow the knee to Him as 'Lord'; we can do no better than follow the Advent Collects: casting off the works of darkness, and putting on the armour of light; reading, marking and learning the Word in holy Scriptures; turning the hearts of the disobedient to the wisdom of the just; and trusting that despite all our sins and hindrances in running the race that is set before us, Jesus, of his bountiful grace and mercy will deliver us.

Chapter III

•

CHRISTMAS

INCARNATION

•

READING FROM THE GOSPEL FOR CHRISTMAS DAY

MEDITATION ON THE GOSPEL FOR CHRISTMAS DAY

•

ARRANGEMENT 6

6   The Nativity
•
Jesus, born of the Virgin Mary

•

READINGS FROM THE EPISTLES FOR ST. STEPHEN, ST. JOHN THE
EVANGELIST, AND THE INNOCENTS.

MEDITATION ON THE EPISTLES FOR ST. STEPHEN, ST. JOHN, AND
THE INNOCENTS

•

ARRANGEMENTS 7, 8, and 9

7   Martyrdom
8   Truth
9   Innocence

•

Jesus standing on the right hand of God

ARRANGEMENT 6—THE NATIVITY

In this Church it is convenient to use the light expansive window to the right of the pulpit to express The Nativity. The light is beginning to dawn amongst the figures of Mary and Joseph and the Christ Child at the base of the arrangement. There we can contemplate the first light of God Incarnate in a dark world, which now has all the potentiality of rich colour and bright light above it.

III CHRISTMAS—INCARNATION

I. THE NATIVITY

Reading from the Gospel for Christmas Day

THE SOURCE OF LIFE AND LIGHT

When all things began, the Word already was. The Word dwelt with God, and what God was, the Word was. The Word, then, was with God at the beginning, and through him all things came to be; no single thing was created without him. All that came to be was alive with his life, AND THAT LIFE WAS THE LIGHT OF MEN. THE LIGHT SHINES ON IN THE DARK, AND THE DARKNESS HAS NEVER QUENCHED IT.

IS HERALDED

There appeared a man named John, sent from God; he came as a witness to testify TO THE LIGHT, that all might become believers through him. He was not himself that light; he came to bear witness of the light. The real light which enlightens every man was even then coming into the world.

AND SHOWN TO MEN

He was in the world; but the world, though it owed its being to him, did not recognise him. He entered his own realm, and his own would not receive his , to those who have yielded him their allegiance, he gave the right to become children of God, not born of any human stock, or by the fleshly desire of a human father, but the offspring of God himself. So the Word became flesh; he came to dwell among us, and we saw his glory, such glory as befits the Father's only Son, full of grace and truth.

The Collect for Christmas Day

Almighty God, who hast given us thy only-begotten Son to take our nature upon him, and as at this time to be born of a pure Virgin; Grant that we being regenerate, and made thy children by adoption and grace, may daily be renewed by thy Holy Spirit; through the same our Lord Jesus Christ, who liveth and reigneth with thee and the same Spirit, ever one God, world without end. Amen.

Meditation on the Gospel for Christmas Day

There was never a time when the Son of God was not. 'All that came to be was alive with His life'. Are we fully aware of this? We came to be when we were conceived and born. Our life at its beginning was alive with His life. And when Jesus Christ, the only Son and Word of God, was conceived by the Holy Spirit and born of the Virgin Mary, the source of our life 'entered His own realm' by Incarnation. At the first Christmas Day 'the real light which lightens every man was even then coming into the world'. So the Word of God became flesh—'He came to dwell among us'—as simple and loving as that. Why do we hide from this real light? Is it because we do not want the dark corners of our self revealed? And is it also because, in a sinful world, the closer we come to the light, the clearer we see the shadow of His Cross and the certainty of our cross for His sake? Christian take courage to come to the Light if this is all that daunts you, for St. Luke records: "And to all He said, 'If anyone wishes to be a follower of mine, he must leave self behind; day after day he must take up his cross, and come with me. Whoever cares for his own safety is lost; but if a man will let himself be lost for my sake, that man is safe. What will a man gain by winning the whole world, at the cost of his true self?" (Luke ix, 23-35) Our life is His, to Him we owe it.

Jesus, born of the Virgin Mary

Herald Angel

Awake! O Church of Christ,
Put on your armor bright,
Arise! and in His Name
Be valiant for the Fight.
An ancient foe attacks
The Honor of His name,
Deceives God's own elect,
And puts God's Son to shame.

The Church

Stand to arms, ye Faithful
With hand upon sword's hilt
Defend that Name for which
Our Martyrs' blood was spilt.
Shall we not vie with them
In this our evil day,
And heed the Call that comes?
We will. Arise! Obey!

Angels

Glory to God on High,
Let Heaven ring with praise,
A valiant army stands,
As in the ancient days.
Arm'd the Christ to follow
Obedient at His word.
Arm'd to defend the Church,
He purchased with His Blood.

The Church

Fall to Prayer, ye Faithful,
Await God's holy Will.
May your suppliant hearts
His Holy spirit fill.
May Vision be reveal'd
To your expectant eyes,
With strength and grace endu'd
To action then arise.

The Vision

"Te Deum laudamus."
Hymn of Triumphant Praise,

Angels and Saints of God
Harmonious song upraise.
But in the midst of Song
Voices in cadence grade;
Lo! at the Throne of God
Is Intercession made.

At God's Right hand, the Christ
Standeth to intercede;
His Church on earth is sad:
He advocates Her need.
Low the Heavenly choir
Prostrate before the Throne
Turn'd from Praise to Prayer—
Prayer, by Christ begun.

Softly from Paradise
Voices of Bless'd ascend.
With the angelic host
Those prayerful voices blend.
Prayers of the Redeem'd
In sweet oblation rise
Odors from the censer
That burns in Paradise.

Seers and holy prophets
Observe the critic's pen
Mar their ancient writings,
God's Message unto men
"Jot and tittle" alter'd
To make the word translate
As suits the scholar's mind
And bring them up to date.

Next follow Gospel scribes,
First guardians of His Name
"Took to set in order"
His Birth, and Life, and fame.
Ah! That "Fair Deposit"
Transmitted with such care
Is no "*historic* fact":
No "*miracle*" is there!

Confessors of the Faith
Who, at the Councils strove
To formulate the Truth
About the Christ they love,
Behold once more the strife,
The heretic abroad
Attacks the Holy Faith,
Defames the Holy Rood.

Martyrs cast their crowns
Before God's Holy Throne
And plead the Cause for which,
In strife, those crowns were won.
Entreating, humbly plead
"If only they were men
They'd give once more their blood
For that dear Faith again."

Priests of the Living Church
Foresee Her altar reft
Of that Divine appeal
The Virgin-born hath left.
Incarnation's glory
Robb'd of Birthright splendour
Invites no more from hearts
Their devout surrender.

Painters of sacred art
See color, light and shade
From their masterpieces
Slowly begin to fade.
Plead for the Madonnas
They painted with such care,
Offerings made to Christ,
Motives unto Prayer.

Writers of sacred verse
Note their inspired theme
Ranked by men to-day,
"Imagination's Dream."
Critics call it "fancy,"
And *poets* they deride,
As though they penn'd those lines

With "muse" not "Christ" their guide

A multitude redeemed
Array'd in spotless white,
Pure through the Blood of Christ,
Who serve Him day and night;
Lift up their eyes to God,
Whose tears God wip'd away;
Join in sweet communion,
In fellowship they pray.

"Defend, O Lord, Thy Church
With Thy perpetual grace
Keep pure Her Faith in Thee,
Reveal to Her Thy Face.
Keep jealous of Thy Name
Thy children who believe,
Defend from foes around,
From their assaults relieve.
Make all to Truth sincere,
The truth as taught of old,
Thy servants arm, O Lord,
And make Thy soldiers bold."

Herald Angel

Arise! O Church of Christ.
Her Cause is lost who waits,
Ye know full well the foe
Already at your gates.
That Vision, 'fore your eyes
Takes shape for you to-day
And she who waits must loose
The fight, through Her delay.

The Church

Lift up your hearts, ye Faithful,
Let us give thanks to God.
Our need is known on high
Through the Incarnate Word
Saints and Angels succour
Our hearts so sadly torn,
Let us in Christ go forth,
Defend the Virgin-Born.

The Rev. Arthur Alcock Baillie (1870-1926)   (*First Published 1909*.)

ARRANGEMENT 8—TRUTH

In this Church the lectern is close to the pulpit. Here the Word of Truth is written
d from here it is read. WHITE the liturgical colour for St. John the Evangelist's Day
used in the arrangement, and the design accentuates the flight and open beak of the
gle. On seeing this picture several people have said: "For the mouth of the Lord hath
oken it".

ARRANGEMENT 9
INNOCENCE

RED is the liturgical colour for martyrs.

Here light red and pink flowers have been used to depict the Feast of The Innocents.

The upward movement of the arrangement connects the same movement of the First Martyr's flowers below with the picture of the Crucifixion right of the pulpit.

ARRANGEMENT 7
MARTYRDOM

The arrangement the Feast of St. Steph is in deep red. The u ward movement of t floral arrangement presses his sufferir offered to God, as looked up to heaven a saw his vision of Jes

CHRISTMAS

2. MARTYRDOM   3. TRUTH.   4. INNOCENCE

Readings from the Epistles for St. Stephen, St. John the Evangelist, and The Innocents.

THE CLAIM TO BE ABLE TO SEE THAT JESUS IS LORD

Stephen . . . saw the glory of God, and Jesus standing at God's right hand. 'Look', he said, 'there is a rift in the sky; I can see the Son of Man standing at God's right hand!'

BRINGS ABOUT THE FIRST MARTYRDOM OF A CHRISTIAN

. . . so they stoned Stephen, and as they did so, he called out, 'Lord Jesus, receive my spirit . . .' (Epistle, St. Stephen's Day)

THE EVANGELIST'S MESSAGE OF TRUTH AND LIGHT ABOUT LIFE

. . . Our theme is the word of life . . . so that you and we together may share in a common life, that life which we share with the Father and his Son Jesus Christ. Here is the message we heard from him and pass on to you: that God is light and in him is no darkness at all . . . if we walk in the light as he himself is in the light, then we share together a common life, and we are being cleansed from every sin by the blood of Jesus his Son. (Epistle, St. John the Evangelist's Day)

REDEMPTION BY INNOCENCY OF LIFE

. . . these were redeemed from among men, being the first-fruits unto God, and to the Lamb. (Epistle, The Innocents Day)

Grant, O Lord, that, in all our sufferings here upon earth for the testimony of thy truth, we may steadfastly look up to heaven, and by faith behold the glory that shall be revealed; and, being filled with the Holy Spirit, may learn to love and bless our persecutors by the example of thy first Martyr Saint Stephen, who prayed for his murderers to thee, O blessed Jesus, who standest at the right hand of God to succour all those that suffer for thee, our only Mediator and Advocate.   Amen.

Meditation on the Epistles for St. Stephen, St. John, and The Innocents

The meaning of the Nativity of the Word, the life and light of men, extends through St. Stephen to the Risen and Ascended Lord Jesus seen through a rift in the sky. Dare we go all the way with Stephen? Do we proclaim whatever personal vision we have of Jesus, at the risk of being stoned? Does not our modern mind sometimes see his death as futile? Or, did it transform Saul, the approver of murder, into Paul, the missionary of Jesus, who bore in his own body the marks of his crucified Lord? Surely the truth is that by believing in Jesus as the Lord of our Life, we share a common life with God, and in Him there is no darkness at all.

But what of the martyrdom of the Innocents of Bethlehem in an attempt to exterminate Jesus? We read that these were redeemed from among men. Innocent or guilty all men die. Even Jesus died, and for us sinners. But redemption and Eternal Life comes by innocency of life and by the innocency of His Life, for all life is made alive with His Life. If we believe that Jesus is Lord, His blood will cleanse us from every sin. In all this, is there not a message of the comforting truth of the loving mercy of God for the innocent and for the sinner? For those who mourn in Aberfan or for those who pray for the repose of the souls of the departed?

THE COLLECT FOR SAINT JOHN THE EVANGELIST'S DAY (*December 27*)

Merciful Lord, we beseech thee to cast thy bright beams of light upon thy Church, that it being enlightened by the doctrine of thy blessed Apostle and Evangelist Saint John may so walk in the light of thy truth, that it may at length attain to the light of everlasting life; through Jesus Christ our Lord.
Amen.

THE COLLECT FOR THE INNOCENT'S DAY (*December 28*)

O Almighty God, who out of the mouths of babies and sucklings hast ordained strength, and madest infants to glorify thee by their deaths; Mortify and kill all vices in us, and so strengthen us by thy grace, that by the innocency of our lives, and the constancy of our faith even unto death, we may glorify thy holy Name; through Jesus Christ our Lord.   Amen

Jesus Standing at God's Right Hand

After accepting that 'Jesus is Lord' and having considered the cry to make His highway straight in preparation for His coming, we read in verse a priest's call to defend the Church's faith in 'Jesus, born of a pure Virgin', composed to confute false teaching early in the 20th century but relevant to a similar attack on the faith today. Now we turn to consider the witness of the first martyr, who died for the sake of the lordship of Jesus. He was honest to God unto death and he said, "Look! there is a rift in the sky; I can see the Son of Man standing at God's right hand!" and at the time he was " . . . filled with the Holy Spirit, and gazing intently up to heaven". He proclaimed what he saw. His was no metaphorical speech. And what he saw was in keeping with what Jesus led his disciples to believe they would see:

" . . . and then they will see the Son of Man coming on a cloud with great power and glory . . . " (Gospel, Advent II).

And what of Jesus at God's right hand? Saint Paul proclaims Him as our Advocate?

"It is Christ—Christ who died, and, more than that, was raised from the dead—who is at God's right hand, and indeed pleads our cause." (Romans VIII.34).

And suggests that we fix our thoughts upon this risen life with Christ:

" . . . aspire to the realm above, where Christ is, seated at the right hand of God, and let your thoughts dwell on that higher realm, not on this earthly life." (Epistle, Easter Day).

Did he think of St. Stephen's vision of Jesus when he wrote to the Ephesians to tell them of his prayer for them?

"I pray that the God of our Lord Jesus Christ, the all-glorious Father, may give you the spiritual powers of wisdom and VISION, by which there comes the knowledge of him. I pray that your inward eyes may be illumined, so that you may know what is the hope to which he calls you, what is the wealth and glory of the share he offers you among his people in their heritage, and how vast the resources of his power open to us who trust in him. They are measured by his strength and the might which he exerted in Christ when he raised him from the dead, when he enthroned him at his right hand in the heavenly realms, far above all government . . . who himself receives the entire fullness of God". (Ephesians i. 17-23 (NEB)).

It is sometimes forgotten today that there are two spiritual powers by which a Christian comes to a knowledge of Jesus as Lord, that of wisdom and that of vision. It is not sufficient to be wise and understanding about the earthly life and work and teachings of Jesus, and put our faith in the exemplary perfection of his manhood, even though this is vital to knowledge of Him and our acceptance of Him as Lord. We need also to have an understanding through the vision of His resurrection and ascension and His place at the right hand of God, and put our faith in Him as truly God, for this also is vital to our knowledge of Him and our acceptance of Him as Lord.

This being so, there can be no question of the Gospel of Jesus being one among many gospels from which men and women can choose their Lord. The profession 'Jesus is Lord' means very little if it does not mean that he is Lord of All. For there is:

"one Lord, one faith, one baptism; one God and Father of all, who is over all and through all and in all". (Epistle, Trinity XVII).

Chapter IV

•

EPIPHANY

MANIFESTATION

•

READINGS FROM THE EPISTLES AND GOSPELS FOR EPIPHANY

MEDITATION ON THE EPISTLES AND GOSPELS FOR EPIPHANY

•

ARRANGEMENTS 10-11

10   Gifts

11   Guidance

•

Do everything in the name of the Lord Jesus

ARRANGEMENT 10. Epiphany—Gifts: These three arrangements depict the Ki
progression is from myrrh, soft blue and violet penitential flowers laced round the
incense, where the arrangement symbolises collective prayer, with individual colu

progress towards the Star (Arr: 11. see op. p.13) near the Nativity window. The
d wood; to gold, seen in golden flowers lifted on silver-pink satin; and on to frank-
nse smoke merging into one as they ascend.

IV. EPIPHANY—MANIFESTATION

1. GIFTS.   2. GUIDANCE

Readings from the Epistles and Gospels for Epiphany

SAINT PAUL SHOWS THE RICHES OF CHRIST TO THE GENTILES

To me . . . he has granted of his grace the privilege of proclaiming to the Gentiles the good news of the unfathomable riches of Christ, and of bringing to light how this hidden purpose was to be put into effect. (Epistle, Epiphany)

THE WISE MEN OFFER THEIR RICHES TO THE CHRIST CHILD

The Star which they had seen at its rising went ahead of them until it stopped above the place where the child lay . . . and (they) offered him gifts: gold, frankincense, and myrrh. (Gospel, Epiphany)

THE MANIFESTATION GIVES GUIDANCE FOR CHRISTIAN BEHAVIOUR

. . . I implore you by God's mercy to offer your very selves to him: a living sacrifice, dedicated and fit for his acceptance, the worship offered by mind and heart . . . (Epistle, Epiphany I) With unflagging energy, in ardour of spirit, serve the Lord. Let hope keep you joyful; in trouble stand firm; persist in prayer. (Epistle, Epiphany II) . . . Do not let evil conquer you, but use good to defeat evil. (Epistle, Epiphany III). . . . Every person must submit to the supreme authorities. There is no authority but by act of God (Epistle, Epiphany IV) . . . Then put on garments that suit God's chosen people . . . Whatever you are doing, whether you speak or act, do everything in the name of the Lord Jesus . . . (Epistle, Epiphany V) . . . Do not be misled: . . . the Son of God appeared for the very purpose of undoing the devil's work (Epistle, Epiphany VI).

The Collect for Epiphany

O God, who by the leading of a star didst manifest thy only-begotten Son to the Gentiles; Mercifully grant, that we, which know thee now by faith, may after this life have the fruition of thy glorious Godhead; through Jesus Christ our Lord. Amen.

The Collect for Epiphany VI

O God, whose blessed Son was manifested that he might destroy the works of the devil, and make us the sons of God, and heirs of eternal life; Grant us, we beseech thee, that, having this hope, we may purify ourselves, even as he is pure; that, when he shall appear again with power and great glory, we may be made like unto him in his eternal and glorious kingdom; where with thee, O Father, and thee, O Holy Spirit, he liveth and reigneth, ever one God, world without end. Amen.

Meditation on the Epistles and Gospels for Epiphany

The manifestation of Jesus as Christ convinces us that 'Jesus is Lord'. In all things he was Lord and especially of his own flesh. The perfection of his human behaviour was and is the guiding star leading to unfathomable riches for man. In our Epistles (in full) the vastness of this store of guidance, which gives divine purpose to man's living, is proclaimed by St. Paul as good news. Yet each separate grace and virtue of a Christian there described is simple and direct in its presentation, difficult and demanding in its execution. Each carrying with it its own particular cross because it has to be lived in the environment of a sinful world. But this is the very purpose of the Son of God's appearing—to undo the devil's work. Are you on the Lord's side in this? If so, when did you last study St. Paul's estimate of Christian behaviour contained in these Epistles and examine yourself accordingly? For he claims that he is revealing to us how the hidden purpose of the Coming of Christ was to be put into effect in our lives. Elsewhere he says: 'Your life is hidden with Christ in God' (Colossians iii.3). All that came to be was and is alive with His life.

Do Everything in The Name of The Lord Jesus

Jesus, being God and one with the Father, is over all and through all and in all. For this reason, though born a Jew, He is shown to the Gentiles. And due homage is offered to His lordship by representative Kings from the Gentile world in token and symbolic gifts of gold, frankincense and myrrh. Gold, the symbol of the wealth of the physical universe is offered because it is His by right: for He is God made man. Frankincense, the symbol of the prayers of men, or the mind of mankind, or noosphere, or the envelope of knowledge encircling the universe is offered because it is His by right: for He is the Incarnate Word of God. And myrrh, the symbol of suffering and death, healing and sacrificial love is offered because it is His by right: for He is the Lamb of God.

Symbolically EVERYTHING is offered to Him because He is Lord of all. But what does this imply for the individual Christian who confesses that 'Jesus is Lord'? It means that he must offer Him his whole life, body, mind and senses, because it is His by right: for He is Lord of his life and God of his salvation—in Him he lives and moves and has his being.

St. Paul tells the Christian to put on garments that suit this calling:

" . . . compassion, kindness, humility, gentleness, patience." Forgiveness, and " . . . to crown all, there must be love, to bind all together and complete the whole . . . " (Colossians iii. 12 & 14 NEB).

There is great danger in believing that we can get-by in our Christian response to the lordship of Jesus by simply offering our gold. For this on its own will only give us a false sense of 'merit'. As far as physical wealth is concerned, St. Paul gives it scant notice. Our moral attitude towards our possessions as gifts from God must be the central feature of our stewardship—that sense of being "filled with gratitude".

The myrrh of compassion, etc. listed above is of far greater importance as a response to the lordship of Jesus. And this depends upon the incense of prayer and revealed knowledge for its sustenance:

" . . . instruct and admonish each other with the utmost wisdom. Sing thankfully in your hearts to God, with psalms and hymns and spiritual songs . . . " (Epistle, Epiphany V).

The lordship of Jesus is seen to affect the Christian in all his behaviour. He must be seen to do everything in the name of the Lord Jesus.

The commitment of the Christian to the lordship of Jesus is sure to founder and become unfruitful unless it is total. In the Book of the Revelation we read:

"To the angel of the Church at Laodicea write: 'These are the words of the Amen, the faithful and true witness, the prime source of all God's creation: I know all your ways; you are neither hot nor cold. How I wish you were either hot or cold! But because you are lukewarm, neither hot nor cold, I will spit you out of my mouth'." (Revelation iii. 14-16 NEB).

What are we to do if we know that we are lukewarm, if we know that we support the teachings of Jesus and that lordship of Jesus which is agreeable to us and reject that which is not? We do well to examine ourselves as to whether this is true discipleship or vanity. And to read again the final words to the Laodiceans:

"All whom I love I reprove and discipline. Be on your mettle therefore and repent. Here I stand knocking at the door; if anyone hears my voice and opens the door, I will come in and sit down to supper with him and he with me. To him who is victorious I will grant a place on my throne, as I myself was victorious and sat down with my Father on his throne. Hear, you who have ears to hear, what the Spirit says to the churches!" (Revelation iii. 19-22 NEB).

The season of Lent which follows will give us the opportunity to turn again unto Him and order our life anew.

Chapter V

•

LENT

FASTING AND SUFFERING

•

READINGS FROM THE LENTEN EPISTLES AND GOSPELS

MEDITATION ON THE LENTEN EPISTLES AND GOSPELS

•

ARRANGEMENTS 12-15

•

Turn ye even unto me, saith the Lord

•

READINGS FROM THE EPISTLE AND GOSPEL FOR GOOD FRIDAY

MEDITATION ON THE EPISTLE AND GOSPEL FOR GOOD FRIDAY

•

ARRANGEMENTS 16 and 17

•

Then at last, to satisfy them, he handed Jesus over to be crucified

ARRANGEMENTS

12	13	14	15
Penitence	Passion	Triumph	Communion

There is no way of understanding the promise of Eternal Life without the penitence and passion of Lent, and the triumph, agony and sacrifice of Holy Week given to us in the Blessed Sacrament of Holy Communion. These messages and the message of Good Friday should therefore stand in a prominent position in front of the congregation and lead to the Altar.

VIOLET and BLUE are liturgical colours for Lent, but Red has been used in the panel representing 'Passion', and the 'Triumph' of Palm Sunday is shown by introducing three palm branches and some lighter colours. In the panel expressing 'Communion' all the colours used for penitence, passion, and triumph have been blended together. The chalice and paten which was displayed to the right of this 'Communion' arrangement is illustrated opposite p. 36.

1. PENITENCE.   2. PASSION.   3. TRIUMPH.   4. COMMUNION.

Readings from the Lenten Epistles and Gospels

BEING MOVED WITH THE SPIRIT OF PENITENCE

. . . 'Do not store up for yourselves treasure on earth . . . Store up treasure in heaven . . . For where your wealth is, there will your heart be also' (Gospel, Ash Wednesday) . . . Turn ye even unto me, saith the Lord, with all your heart . . . And rend your heart, and not your garments (Lesson, Ash Wednesday.RV.)

HOW TO DEAL WITH THE TEMPTER

. . . Jesus was then led away by the Spirit into the wilderness . . . the tempter approached him . . . If thou be the Son of God (twice) . . . (and) all these will I give you if . . . But Jesus said, Begone, Satan; Scripture says, 'you shall do homage to the Lord your God and worship him alone'. (Gospel, Lent I).

THE PASSION AND TRIUMPH OF THE CROSS

. . . We pass on to you the tradition of the way we must live to please God; you are indeed already following it, but we beg you to do so yet more thoroughly . . . This is the will of God, that you should be holy (Epistle, Lent II) . . . try to be like him (Jesus) and live in love as Christ loved you and gave himself up on your behalf as an offering and sacrifice . . . As Christians you are light. Live like men who are at home in daylight, for where light is there all goodness springs up, all justice and truth (Epistle, Lent III) . . . Let your bearing towards one another arise out of your life in Christ Jesus . . . he humbled himself, and in obedience accepted even death—death on a cross. Therefore God has raised him to the heights . . . that . . . every tongue confess, 'Jesus is Lord', to the glory of God the Father (Epistle, Sunday next before Easter).

THE COMMUNION AND FELLOWSHIP OF THE CROSS

. . . Every time you eat this bread and drink this cup, you proclaim the death of the Lord, until he comes (Epistle, Thursday before Easter).

THE COLLECT FOR ASH WEDNESDAY

Almighty and everlasting God, who hatest nothing that thou hast made, and dost forgive the sins of all them that are penitent; Create and make in us new and contrite hearts, that we worthily lamenting our sins, and acknowledging our wretchedness, may obtain of thee, the God of all mercy, perfect remission and forgiveness; through Jesus Christ our Lord. Amen.

THE COLLECT FOR THE SUNDAY NEXT BEFORE EASTER

Almighty and everlasting God, who, of thy tender love towards mankind, hast sent thy Son, our Saviour Jesus Christ, to take upon him our flesh, and to suffer death upon the cross, that all mankind should follow the example of his great humility; Mercifully grant that we may both follow the example of his patience, and also be made partakers of his resurrection; through the same Jesus Christ our Lord. Amen.

THE COLLECT FOR THE INSTITUTION OF HOLY COMMUNION

O Lord, who in a wonderful Sacrament hast left us a memorial of thy passion: Grant us so to reverence the holy mysteries of the Body and Blood, that we may ever know within ourselves the fruit of thy redemption; who livest and reignest with the Father, in the unity of the Holy Spirit, one God, world without end. Amen.

Meditation on the Lenten Epistles and Gospels

Does the Spirit invite you along the path of penitence? If he does, and you begin to tread it, you can be sure that you will find a wilderness there and also the tempter. No one else can face this trial for you. Your freedom depends on it. But Jesus will face it with you, and He will know your struggle for He has a fellowship with your predicament. And what is more God will not allow you to be tempted above that you are able, and he will with the temptation show you the way of escape. The path of repentance is worth it, since it brings you to the light, and where light is, there all goodness springs up, all justice and truth. Before you move on with Him to Good Friday, the Bread and Wine are there for the strengthening and refreshing of your soul.

Turn Ye Even Unto Me

For everyone of us there come times of experience in the wilderness, where the comforts of life are lacking, or hardships prevail, or doubts of intellect and temptations assail our inmost being. Though Jesus is Lord, He too was led by the Spirit into the wilderness and tempted in all things as we are. By strength of human will and perception of God's will for the perfection of man He did no sin, and the tempter turned away from Him and left Him. The fellowship of His victory is ours if we turn to Him as Lord. We read that:

"God keeps faith, and he will not allow you to be tested above your powers, but when the test comes he will at the same time provide a way out, by enabling you to sustain it." (Epistle, Trinity IX).

Our certainty of the lordship of Jesus is our way out and to Him we can always turn:

"Turn ye even unto me, saith the Lord, with all your heart . . . "

We notice once again that our surrender must be total—with all our heart.

And what if the tempter succeeds and we fall? We know how often this is the predicament in which we find ourselves. In this state also we can with a penitent heart 'turn unto Him as Lord' and in Him we will find forgiveness.

Some who read this may feel that it is too late, they have fallen too often; or become too involved in the comforting wealth of the physical world, and in many cases the stimulating wealth of the intellectual world of humanism. But it is never too late. Jesus knew the mind and the nature of the Father when he answered the question:

"Lord, how often am I to forgive my brother if he goes on wronging me? As many as seven times? Jesus replied, 'I do not say seven times; I say seventy times seven'." (Gospel, Trinity XXII).

By his own confession, who can have sinned more against the lordship of Jesus than St. Paul before his conversion? Yet he was chosen by the same Jesus whom he had persecuted to publish the gospel of forgiveness of sins.

"'Tell me, Lord, who you are'; and the Lord replied, 'I am Jesus whom you are persecuting. But now, rise to your feet and stand upright. I have appeared to you for a purpose: to appoint you my servant and witness, to testify both to what you have seen and to what you shall yet see of me. I will rescue you from this people and from the Gentiles to whom I am sending you. I send you to open their eyes and turn them from darkness to light, from the dominion of Satan to God, so that, by trust in me, they may obtain forgiveness of sins, and a place with those whom God has made his own.'" (Acts xxvi.15b-18. NEB).

And St. Paul's case was no isolated one in Christian history, examples could be given from the lives of St. Augustine, St. Cyprian and countless others. So often it has occurred that he, to whom God has had to extend the greatest forgiveness through Jesus, has in thanksgiving offered most fully his heart and his life to the confession that 'Jesus is Lord'.

Rest assured then that it is never too late to turn unto the Lord your God. You may have allowed many seasons of Lent to pass without making much effort to 'turn'. Over and over again you may have attempted to 'turn' and failed to sustain a complete acceptance of Jesus as Lord of your life. Yet through His Church each Lent He will not cease to call you to turn to Him.

The practical religion in the Epistle of St. James tells us what to expect and what is required of us when we do turn:

" . . . whenever you have to face trials of many kinds, count yourself supremely happy, in the knowledge that such testing of your faith breeds fortitude, and if you give fortitude full play you will go on to complete a balanced character that will fall short in nothing. If any of you falls short in wisdom, he should ask God for it and it will be given him, for God is a generous giver who neither refuses nor reproaches anyone. But he must ask in faith, without a doubt in his mind; for the doubter is like a heaving sea ruffled by the wind. A man of that kind must not expect the Lord to give him anything; he is double-minded, and never can keep a steady course." (James i.2-8. NEB).

MAUNDY THURSDAY (Communion) — To represent the Institution of the Blessed Sacrament our illustration shows the Chalice and Paten at the Ancient Chapelry of All Saints, Dewlish for the past 350-400 years.

Right: ARRANGEMENT 17—Sacrifice.
Below: ARRANGEMENTS 16 & 17
both representing GOOD FRIDAY.
(See also opposite p.4 for ARRANGE-
MENT 16.) Here the deep Red of sacrifice and suffering opens the door of
the beholder's vision to the joyous
colours of the Easter season in the
chancel and sanctuary.

5. SACRIFICE

Readings from the Epistle and Gospel for Good Friday

SHADOWS AS WELL AS DARKNESS ARE BROUGHT TO LIGHT

For the law contains but a shadow, and no true image, of the good things which were to come; it provides the same sacrifices year after year, and with these it can never bring the worshippers to perfection for all time. . . . Christ offered for all time one sacrifice for sins . . . For by one offering he has perfected for all time those who are thus consecrated . . . So . . . the blood of Jesus makes us free to enter boldy into the sanctuary of the new, living way which he has opened for us through the curtain, the way of his flesh. We have, moreover, a great priest set over the household of God; so let us make our approach in sincerity of heart and full assurance of faith, our guilty hearts sprinkled clean, our bodies washed with pure water. Let us be firm and unswerving in the confession of our hope, for the Giver of the promise may be trusted. We ought to see how each of us may best arouse others to love and active goodness, not staying away from our meetings, as some do, but rather encouraging one another, all the more because you see the Day drawing near. (Epistle, Good Friday).

BY THE CROSS OF JESUS

. . . 'Crucify your king?' said Pilate. 'We have no king but Caesar', the Jews replied. Then at last, to satisfy them, he handed Jesus over to be crucified. (Gospel, Good Friday).

The First Two Collects for Good Friday

Almighty God, we beseech thee graciously to behold this thy family, for which our Lord Jesus Christ was contented to be betrayed, and given up into the hands of wicked men, and to suffer death upon the cross, who now liveth and reigneth with thee and the Holy Spirit, ever one God, world without end. Amen.

Almighty and everlasting God, by whose Spirit the whole body of the Church is governed and sanctified; Receive our supplications and prayers, which we offer before thee for all estate of men in thy holy Church, that every member of the same, in his vocation and ministry, may truly and godly serve thee; through our Lord and Saviour Jesus Christ. Amen.

Meditation on the Epistle and Gospel for Good Friday

Time takes its corruptive toll of the stones and mortar of any buildings. Without periodical restoration they become a mere shadow of what they were. So it is with out human actions according to the foundations of our faith. After generations of familiarity traditional beliefs slide into the shadows of vanity and abuse.

The truth of sacrifice as a way of redemption in a world of sin was clear to Abraham; and his faith was established for many generations in a covenant. It provided the same sacrifices year after year. As time extended the sacrifices became so lost in the shadows of an impersonal piety that Job, in the midst of the system, was moved to re-utter the great question-mark of the Old Testament: 'How can a man be just before God?'

Later, on a Good Friday, Jesus answered the question in his own Passion and Death on a Cross. He offered for all time one sacrifice for sins. But has this become an impersonal truth for us? Does the message of the Cross really prompt our every action? He made the sacrifice for us sinners. Do we make confession of our sins as well as our faith? There is opportunity to do this in the Holy Communion. Have we let our preparation for confession slip into the shadows by disuse?

Then at last, 'to satisfy them', he handed Jesus over to be crucified

Pilate was not to know that he was offering to the people a means of satisfaction which was to become a sacrifice for the sins of all.

Jesus had said:

"I am the bread of life . . . I am speaking of the bread that comes down from heaven, which a man may eat, and never die. I am that living bread which has come down from heaven: if anyone eats this bread he shall live for ever. Moreover, the bread which I will give is my own flesh; I give it for the life of the world." (John vi.48-51. NEB).

And this discourse which Jesus had with the Jews is preceded in St. John's Gospel by an account of the feeding of the five thousand. The Authorised Version of St. Mark's account of the same feeding of the five thousand may help our thoughts about the lordship of Jesus. The word 'satisfy' is used in the translation:

"And his disciples answered him, from whence can a man satisfy these men with bread here in the wilderness?" (Gospel, Lent IV, and Trinity XXV. (A.V.)).

There can be a great deal of difference between feeding and satisfying, as Jesus explains to the Jews in St. John's account of the discourse:

"This is the bread which came down from heaven; and it is not like the bread which our fathers ate; they are dead, but whoever eats this bread shall live for ever". (John vi.58).

Jesus is Lord, and for this reason His sacrifice will in the fullest sense satisfy men. And just as when:

"Jesus grew up he advanced in wisdom and in favour with God and men" (Luke ii.52b.NEB),

so also God the Father was satisfied with His Son's sacrifice for the sins of men, as was prophesied by Isaiah:

"He shall see the travail of his soul, and shall be satisfied: by his knowledge shall my righteous servant justify many; for he shall bear their iniquities". (Isaiah lii.11).

Truly the death of Jesus Christ upon the Cross for our redemption was not only a full, perfect, and sufficient sacrifice and oblation, for the sins of the whole world; it was also a full, perfect, and sufficient satisfaction for the sins of the whole world; both to God and for men.

Corregio's picture of the Crucifixion has this inscription:

I HAVE BORN THESE THINGS FOR THEE—
WHAT HAST THOU DONE FOR ME?

A statement of fact and a challenging question. A question which demands an answer from everyone. And because Jesus is Lord an answer will be required from all. It is said that a mountain challenges men to attempt to climb it because it is there. By the same analogy but with an eternal weight of emphasis an answer to the question, 'What hast thou done for me?' challenges all, because He hung there on the Cross. ECCE HOMO.

Once again we are bound to be struck by the lordship of His total offering of Himself for us and all mankind. If Jesus is Lord there can be no half measures for Him. Equally if we confess that 'Jesus is Lord' there should be no half measures with us.

Because the mountain is there we will go on climbing it in an endeavour to reach the top, however many times we fail. In the same manner, because we fail so often to match up our life to the confession that 'Jesus is Lord', this is no reason to turn from Him and seek an easier climb. For He is still there. We may try to avoid Him, but in the last analysis we cannot. He is our only hope of making satisfaction before God and finding redemption from the sins which separate us from God.

The Christian ought not to allow himself to be deluded into thinking that satisfaction can be found elsewhere than in Jesus because modern thinking is tolerant towards all faiths. St. Peter's words recorded in the Acts of the Apostles are uncompromising:

"This Jesus is the stone rejected by the builders which has become the keystone—and you are the builders. There is no salvation in any-one else at all, for there is no other name under heaven granted to men, by which we may receive salvation". (Acts iv.11 and 12. NEB).

Chapter VI
•

EASTER

RESURRECTION

•

READINGS FROM THE EPISTLES AND GOSPELS FOR EASTER EVEN
AND EASTER DAY

MEDITATION ON THE EPISTLES AND GOSPELS FOR EASTER EVEN
AND EASTER DAY

•

ARRANGEMENTS 18, 19, and 20

18   Life through death
19 & 20 The Gate of Everlasting Life

•

READINGS FROM THE EPISTLES AND GOSPELS FOR EASTER I AND II

MEDITATION ON THE EPISTLES AND GOSPELS FOR EASTER I AND II

•

ARRANGEMENTS 21 and 22

21   Pureness of Living
22   Exemplary Living

•

MEDITATION ON THE EPISTLES AND GOSPELS FOR EASTER III, IV and V

READINGS FROM THE ESPISTLES AND GOSPELS FOR EASTER III, IV and V

•

ARRANGEMENTS 23, 24 and 25

23   Joy of Living
24   Glory of Living
25   Victory of Living

•

Jesus is Risen

Above: ARRANGEMENT 18—The Empty Tomb. Here are seen the stone rolled away, the linen, the angel, and Easter garden. Below ARRANGEMENTS 19 and 20—The Gate of Everlasting Life

VI. EASTER—RESURRECTION

1. LIFE THROUGH DEATH.

2. THE GATE OF EVERLASTING LIFE.

Readings from the Epistles and Gospels for Easter Even and Easter Day

SUFFERING AND DEATH AS A BASIS OF MORAL CONDUCT AND A MEANS OF GRACE

It is better to suffer for well-doing, if such should be the will of God, than for doing wrong. For Christ also died for our sins once and for all. He, the just, suffered for the unjust, to bring us to God (Epistle, Easter Even).

. . . When evening fell . . . Joseph took the body (of Jesus), wrapped it in a clean linen sheet, and laid it in his own unused tomb, which he had cut out of the rock; he then rolled a large stone against the entrance, and went away . . . The Pharisees came in a body to Pilate . . . 'Will you give orders for the grave to be made secure?; . . . So they went and made the grave secure; they sealed the stone, and left the guard in charge (Gospel, Easter Even).

WHICH IS HIDDEN BUT RISEN TO A NEW WAY OF LIVING

Were you not raised to live with Christ? Then aspire to the realm above, where Christ is, seated at the right hand of God, and let your thoughts dwell on that higher realm, not on this earthly life. I repeat, you died; and your life lies hidden with Christ in God . . . (Epistle, Easter Day).

. . . Then the disciple who had reached the tomb first went in too, and he saw and believed; until then they had not understood the scriptures, which showed that he must rise from the dead (Gospel, Easter Day).

THE COLLECT FOR EASTER EVEN

Grant, O Lord, that as we are baptised into the death of thy blessed Son our Saviour Jesus Christ, so by continual mortifying our corrupt affections we may be buried with him; and that through the grave, and gate of death, we may pass to our joyful resurrection; for his merits, who died, and was buried, and rose again for us, thy Son Jesus Christ our Lord. Amen.

THE COLLECT FOR EASTER DAY

Almighty God, who through thine only-begotten Son Jesus Christ hast overcome death, and opened unto us the gate of everlasting life; We humbly beseech thee, that, as by thy special grace preventing us thou dost put into our minds good desires, so by thy continual help we may bring the same to good effect; through Jesus Christ our Lord, who liveth and reigneth with thee and the Holy Spirit, ever one God, world without end. Amen.

Meditation on the Epistles and Gospels for Easter Even and Easter Day

Before we cross the chancel steps to approach the altar, we cannot begin to understand the risen life of Eastertide until we have pondered the experience of Jesus' followers on Easter Even. The grave is silent, sealed, and guarded. Where can they look for comfort? Most of us have stood by the grave of a loved-one, and prayed that some comfort might fill our empty hearts. Mary Magdala was there, and the other Mary, sitting opposite the grave. We know their desolation. Why should he, the just, suffer for the unjust? We return to visit the tomb (as though it were early on the Sunday morning). Before we reach the sanctuary steps we can see that the tomb is empty. But where have they laid him? The flowers, in such beautiful order and as clean as the linen lying there, seem to indicate the excitement of renewed life. But life of a different kind. We turn to the altar seeking a higher realm of life, and there we see the portal of all life, even life through death. Jesus is indeed Lord, and there pours into our heart the faith that God has raised him from the dead. Salvation is ours through him, because all life takes on a new meaning. We see our own life hidden in him. In this spiritual communion at the altar we are reminded of the refreshment and strength we have so often received in the Holy Communion.

3. PURENESS OF LIVING.   4. EXEMPLARY LIVING.

Readings from the Epistles and Gospels for Easter I and II

THE PROMISE TO BELIEVERS OF ETERNAL LIFE

. . . The victory that defeats the world is our faith, for who is victor over the world but he who believes that Jesus is the Son of God? . . . The witness is this: that God has given us eternal life, and that this life is found in his Son. He who possesses the Son has life indeed; he who does not possess the Son of God has not that life (Epistle, Easter I).

BRINGS PURITY THROUGH REMISSION OF SINS IN THE FELLOWSHIP OF GOD'S PEACE

. . . Jesus repeated, 'Peace be with you!', and then said, 'As the Father sent me, so I send you'. He then breathed on them, saying, 'Receive the Holy Spirit! If you forgive any man's sins, they stand forgiven; if you pronounce them unforgiven, unforgiven they remain'. (Gospel, Easter I).

AND AFTER THE EXAMPLE OF THE MOST HOLY LIFE OF JESUS

. . . I am the good shepherd; I know my own sheep, and my sheep know me—as the Father knows me and I know the Father —and I lay down my life for the sheep (Gospel, Easter II).

WE MUST ENDEAVOUR TO LIVE EACH DAY

For it is a fine thing if a man endure the pain of undeserved suffering because God is in his thoughts . . . To that you were called, because Christ suffered on your behalf, and thereby left you an example; it is for you to follow in his steps . . . You were straying like sheep, but now you have turned towards the Shepherd and Guardian of your souls (Epistle, Easter II).

The Collect for Easter I

Almighty Father, who hast given thine only Son to die for our sins, and to rise again for our justification ; Grant us so to put away the leaven of malice and wickedness, that we may always serve thee in pureness of living and truth ; through the merits of the same thy Son Jesus Christ our Lord.   Amen.

The Collect for Easter II

Almighty God, who hast given thine only Son to be unto us both a sacrifice for sin, and also an example of godly life ; give us grace that we may always most thankfully receive that his inestimable benefit, and also daily endeavour ourselves to follow the blessed steps of his most holy life ; through the same Jesus Christ our Lord.   Amen.

‡

Meditation on the Epistles and Gospels for Easter I and II

By faith we possess Jesus and his life with all its healing and power extending to us. His life through death grows upon us; influencing us, to seek purity of living for ourselves and all mankind, and to follow his exemplary living through joy and glory to ultimate victory. We begin our communion with this Eternal Life in the same way as we begin the Holy Communion. That is, with a prayer for purity. His Birth by a pure Virgin will help us. In the stable we find the same peaceful approach to us as accompanies the breath of forgiveness in the Gospel. The next step is to seek to know Jesus as he knows us. With so many resources for doing this, have we used them fully? This parable and picture of Jesus as the Good Shepherd carries us forward, as here he carries the lamb. And the lamb trusts him with his life. However far we have strayed from Jesus, we are called again. And we can, if we will, turn towards a life in which we acclaim that 'Jesus is Lord', the Shepherd and Guardian of our soul. With this in our thoughts we can, in confidence of God's Will, suffer the pain of undeserved suffering more easily.

44

ARRANGEMENT 21—Pureness of Living.

In the South wall of the chancel and within the sanctuary is this stained glass window showing the Nativity. Yellow is the predominant colour in the window and this is used in the simple arrangement expressing 'pureness of living' which is the message of Easter 1.

ARRANGEMENT 22—Exemplary Living.

Behind choir stalls, in the South wall of the chancel, is this stained glass window showing the Good Shepherd. The arrangement in Red for self-sacrifice blends with the window to express 'Exemplary Living', for Easter II.

Right: These two arrangements develop the colours used for Lent and Good Friday nearby into an expression of the Joy (23) and the Glory (24) of Living, which are the messages of Easter III and IV.

Left: The three arrangements are seen together in this picture with the Joy and Glory of Living leading up to the Victory of Living. In place of the usual curtain behind these panels a grey corrugated paper was used, as in the panels depicting Lent.

ARRANGEMENT 25—The Victory of Living.

ARRANGEMENT 28—Love Ascending into the Heavens.

This is an enlargement of one of the three arrangements for Ascension Day seen opposite p.49 and really belongs to Chapter VII. But its position here is not out of place because the message of Ascensiontide is closely related to the message of the Victory of Living and the design of the arrangement has much the same 'line' as Arrangement 25 (overleaf).

Students of the works of Teilhard de Chardin might find it interesting to compare the line of this arrangement with his diagram in 'The Future of Man', which demonstrates man's progress in relation to God. Especially if the same design of thought is allowed to include the progress of man in past history in relation to God.

5. THE JOY OF LIVING.   6. THE GLORY OF LIVING.

7. THE VICTORY OF LIVING.

Readings from the Epistles and Gospels for Easter III, IV and V

THE BELIEVER'S SUFFERING TURNED INTO JOY

Dear friends, I beg you . . . to abstain from the lusts of the flesh which are at war with the soul. Let all your behaviour be such as even pagans can recognise as good, and then, whereas they malign you as criminals now, they will come to see for themselves that you live good lives . . . Submit yourselves to every human institution for the sake of the Lord . . . For it is the will of God that by your good conduct you should put ignorance and stupidity to silence. Live as free men; not as though your freedom were there to provide a screen for wrongdoing, but as slaves in God's service. Give due honour to everyone . . . (Epistle, Easter III).

. . . You will weep and mourn, but the world will be glad. But though you will be plunged in grief, your grief will be turned to joy . . . For the moment you are sad at heart; but I shall see you again, and then you will be joyful, and no one shall rob you of your joy (Gospel, Easter III).

AS THE HOLY SPIRIT REVEALS TO HIM THE GLORY OF JESUS

. . . But now I am going away to him that sent me . . . However, when he comes who is the Spirit of truth, he will guide you into all the truth . . . He will glorify me, for everything that he makes known to you he will draw from what is mine . . . (Gospel, Easter IV).

IN WHICH HE WILL FIND THE VICTORY OF LIVING

Only be sure that you act on the message and do not merely listen; for that would be to mislead yourselves . . . (Epistle, Easter V).

(Jesus said) . . . 'I have told you all this so that in me you may find peace. In the world you will have trouble. But courage! The victory is mine; I have conquered the world' (Gospel, Easter V).

The Collect for Easter III

Almighty God, who shewest to them that be in error the light of thy truth, to the intent that they may return into the way of righteousness; Grant unto all them that are admitted into the fellowship of Christ's Religion, that they may eschew those things that are contrary to their profession, and follow all such things as are agreeable to the same; through our Lord Jesus Christ. Amen.

The Collect for Easter IV

O Almighty God, who alone canst order the unruly wills and affections of sinful men; Grant unto thy people, that they may love the thing which thou commandest, and desire that which thou dost promise; that so, among the sundry and manifold changes of the world, our hearts may surely there be fixed, where true joys are to be found; through Jesus Christ our Lord. Amen.

The Collect for Easter V

O Lord, from whom all good things do come; Grant to us thy humble servants, that by thy holy inspiration we may think those things that be good, and by thy merciful guiding may perform the same; through our Lord Jesus Christ. Amen.

Meditation on the Epistles and Gospels for Easter
III, IV and V

We all need a foundation stone from which our 'living' springs. Where can we find one which is eternal and yet can be known in part in temporal life? As Christians we believe and know that Jesus is Risen from a temporal death. The eternal truth which must be applied to all our living is that there was never a time when Jesus, the Son of God, was not; nor will there ever be a time when he is not, for he is Risen. Our joy, glory, and victory of living must therefore be found in him. It is the foundation of our life that 'Jesus is Lord'. In every aspect of his pure and exemplary incarnate life there is joy, glory and victory in his peace with the will of God even unto death. Whatever happens to us in the service of our Lord, even pain, suffering or death, no one shall rob us of our joy in him. In his life we glorify God and conquer.

Jesus is Risen

From the teaching and faith that Jesus is Lord by virtue of His earthly life, we turn to contemplate the teaching and faith that Jesus is Lord by virtue of His Resurrection and Ascension.

"He showed himself to these men (the Apostles) after his death, and gave ample proof that he was alive: over a period of forty days he appeared to them and taught them about the kingdom of God." (Epistle, Ascension Day).

There are many witnesses of His Resurrection and their record can be found in the eight Gospels appointed for the season of Eastertide. The world court of mankind still attempts to deny this statement that the independent witness of so many is ample proof. Yet the defence of this early witness and faith has been championed by the Church's baptised members for almost 2,000 years. And His Risen Life has been seen in the lives of those who have confessed Him as Lord, changed from darkness to light, from sorrow and despair to joy and hope, from fear and hate to confidence and love, from a life of selfishness and greed to a life dedicated to the glory of God, from a life imprisoned in the flesh of man to a life with the spirit of man victorious over the flesh. No one can deny the evidence of this transformation in the lives of many throughout the history of the Christian Church. And all who have been thus changed have confessed that Jesus is Lord of their lives and have believed that He is risen from the dead. What reasoning man could proclaim Jesus as Lord of his life, if he believed that He died on Calvary and did not rise from the dead? The alternative to this faith which brings joy and hope and divine love into the life of man might be expressed in the verses of another poem published in 1909 as a defence against those who denied the Resurrection of Jesus.

IF CHRIST IS NOT

Bethlehem's Star has set,
        Shepherds sleep,
        Wise men sleep,
And all the world is wet
        Wet with Tears,
Tears that cry, "Forsaken"
        And Fears
In sad hearts awaken
        And cry
        In agony
If Christ is not.

Calvary has no Cross,
        Satan reigns,
        Death gains,
And all the world is wet,
        Wet with Tears,
Tears that say, "Bereaved"
        And Fears
Fearful and unrelieved
        Sin! Sin! Sin!
        Nought to win
If Christ is not.

Joseph's Tomb lies empty
        Pious fraud!
        Man out-lawed.
And all the world is wet,
        Wet with Tears,
Tears that cry, "Deluded"
        And Fears
Of a soul denuded
        No Resurrection!
        No Resurrection!
If Christ is not.

No cloud o'er Olivet
        No History
        No Mystery,
And all the world is wet,
        Wet with Tears,
No interceding cry.
        And Fears
No Advocate on high.
        Hearts bleed,
        Cold creed,
If Christ is not.

The Rev. A. A. Baillie (1870-1926)

Chapter VII

•

ASCENSIONTIDE

EARTH AND HEAVEN

•

READINGS FROM THE EPISTLES AND GOSPELS FOR ASCENSIONTIDE

MEDITATION ON THE EPISTLES AND GOSPELS FOR ASCENSIONTIDE

•

ARRANGEMENTS 26, 27, 28 and 29

26— 28   Love ascending into the Heavens

29   Love ascending and descending

•

The Lord worked with them and confirmed their
words by the miracles that followed

ARRANGEMENT 29—
Love Ascending and Descending.

Above : This window is high above the d[oor]
at the West end of the North side aisle. T[he]
descending right arm of the arrangem[ent]
leads the eye of the beholder down to [the]
Whitsuntide windows in the North wall.[In]
this way the two seasons are linked with [the]
message of the ascent and descent of Go[d's]
Love.

Left : This window is at the West end of [the]
Church under the Tower. The steps [of]
Ascension from earth to heaven are she[wn]
in the penitential VIOLET colour at the b[ase]
of the Font, the same colour touched w[ith]
a little yellow on top of the Font, lead[ing]
up to the Trinity green, the creamy yell[ow]
and the bright blue in the window abo[ve]
(See also opposite p.45 for the wind[ow]
arrangement—No. 28).

ARRANGEMENTS 26, 27 & 28—
Love Ascending into the Heavens.

VII. ASCENSIONTIDE—ASCENSION

1. LOVE ASCENDING INTO THE HEAVENS.
2. LOVE ASCENDING AND DESCENDING.

Readings from the Epistles and Gospels for Ascensiontide

AFTER COMMISSIONING THE APOSTLES JESUS ASCENDS TO THE FATHER

'. . . You will receive power when the Holy Spirit comes upon you; and you will bear witness for me in Jerusalem, and all over Judaea and Samaria, and away to the ends of the earth.' When he (Jesus) had said this, as they watched, he was lifted up, and a cloud removed him from their sight (Epistle, Ascension Day).

. . . Afterwards while the eleven were at table he appeared to them and reproached them for their incredulity and dullness, because they had not believed those who had seen him risen from the dead. Then he said to them: 'Go forth to every part of the world, and proclaim the Good News to the whole creation . . .' So after talking with them the Lord Jesus was taken up into heaven, and he took his seat at the right hand of God; but they went out to make their proclamation everywhere, and the Lord worked with them and confirmed their words by the miracles that followed (Gospel, Ascension Day).

AND ONE OF THE APOSTLES, PETER, PASSES ON THIS COMMUNION OF LOVE TO OTHERS

. . . Above all, keep your love for one another at full strength, because love cancels innumerable sins. Be hospitable to one another without complaining. Whatever gift each of you may have received, use it in service to one another, like good stewards dispensing the grace of God in its varied forms . . . In all things so act that the glory may be God's through Jesus Christ (Epistle, Sunday after Ascension Day).

49

Grant, we beseech thee, Almighty God, that like as we do believe thy only-begotten Son our Lord Jesus Christ to have ascended into the heavens; so we may also in heart and mind thither ascend, and with him continually dwell, who liveth and reigneth with thee and the Holy Spirit, one God, world without end.   Amen.

THE COLLECT FOR THE SUNDAY AFTER ASCENSION DAY

O God the King of glory, who hast exalted thine only Son Jesus Christ with great triumph unto thy kingdom in heaven; We beseech thee, leave us not comfortless; but send to us thine Holy Spirit to comfort us, and exalt us unto the same place whither our Saviour Christ is gone before, who liveth and reigneth with thee and the Holy Spirit, one God, world without end.
Amen.

Meditation on the Epistles and Gospels for Ascensiontide

It is not sufficient for the Christian to have faith in the Resurrection and Ascension of Jesus, he must also use his life and influence to bear witness. The commission to do this comes from Christ at his Ascension through his Apostles and their successors.

Today, although there are countless believers all over the earth, less and less of them are prepared to confess their faith openly. Yet the believer is called to proclaim his faith. Should he not follow the pattern of Jesus and reproach men for their incredulity and dullness?

Toleration has raced ahead of mission, the greater part of the evangelising zeal of the Christian today is dormant and unexpressed. It is pushed into the shadows and not brought to the light. But the Christian should never fail in his witness for Christ in the interests of toleration.

Jesus is Ascended, but his love still stretches down to cover, therefore above all, our love for others should be kept at full strength. Love covers all!

The Lord Worked With Them

The faith of the Christian in the Ascension of Jesus carries with it a vision in which 'Jesus is Lord' in a realm far higher than we have considered so far. A realm in which there is to be a redemption of our body:

"We wait for God to make us his sons and set our whole body free" (Romans viii.23b. NEB).

And this redemption we can already know in part by the gift of the Spirit in Baptism. For this is the beginning of the quickening of our mortal bodies. The beginning of a death unto sin and a new birth unto righteousness:

"If the Spirit of him who raised Jesus from the dead dwells within you, then the God who raised Christ Jesus from the dead will also give new life to your mortal bodies through his indwelling Spirit" (Romans viii.11.NEB).

The lordship of Jesus was such that when He ascended, His nature was not separated from human nature. Rather His manhood was taken up into the Godhead. And therefore He is still at one with man. And this is the measure of His lordship and the completeness of the atonement He has made with God for mankind. In it salvation is found for all who confess that 'Jesus is Lord'. And such salvation carries with it a share in his glory:

"We . . . are citizens of heaven, and from heaven we expect our deliverer to come, the Lord Jesus Christ. He will transform the body belonging to our humble state, and give it a form like that of his own resplendent body, by the very power which enables him to make all things subject to himself." (Philippians iii.21.NEB).

The lordship of the Ascended Jesus also makes Him the believer's Advocate in heaven when he falls into sin:

"Should anyone commit a sin, we have one to plead our cause with the Father, Jesus Christ, and he is just. He is himself the remedy for the defilement of our sins, not ours only but the sins of all the world." (I John ii.1. NEB).

Once again we find that His lordship in the forgiveness of sins, as in all else, is total. There can be no partial lordship.

If there were no need for a Final Judgement, there would be no need for redemption. The New Testament makes it quite clear that the glory of Jesus will be shown in His judgements as in His redemption. In judgement Jesus is to be Lord. And because

He is so completely identified with man in His lordship, the love or lack of it shown by men to men in all their actions will be the measure by which all will be judged.

This then is the sense in which Jesus as Lord works with the believer, and the way in which He expects the believer to work with Him. He is Lord of everything, every creature, and every human being of whatever colour, creed, or nationality. And as Lord and God he is Love, and loves all. The believer's work under Him must be to shew this love to all without exception. What greater task than this could a man be called to do? It is difficult in the extreme. It requires the zeal of the missionary, and the courage of the martyr, and above and before all this a knowledge of Jesus, His life, His teachings, His healing, His death, His resurrection and ascension, His presence in the Blessed Sacrament. This is all essential to the confession that 'Jesus is Lord'. In general this is the pattern of life for the Christian. But for particular reference all the Epistles and Gospels of the Church's Year should be read. This guidance is best heard Sunday by Sunday within the Eucharistic liturgy. And for this reason regular attendance at public worship is a matter of obligation for the believer.

For many, worship in church has become an agreeable extra to be indulged in when there is time, and when it does not conflict with other commitments.

What is the remedy? The faithful must be—honest to God. They must ask themselves fairly and squarely: Do they or don't they confess that 'Jesus is Lord'. If they do, then the corporate worship of the Church becomes an obligation in their life and not an optional extra. If they do not, it will remain for them an optional extra. And even as such the welcoming door of the church should be open because Jesus made Himself the servant of all even though He was Lord of all. His love and forgiveness is given freely to all who approach Him. He is always available however frequent or infrequent is man's application to Him for mercy or help. This is the measure of His lordship.

Chapter VIII

•

WHITSUNTIDE

RENEWAL

•

READINGS FROM THE EPISTLE AND GOSPEL FOR WHIT SUNDAY

MEDITATION ON THE EPISTLES AND GOSPELS FOR WHITSUNTIDE

•

ARRANGEMENTS 30, 31 and 32

•

Peter commanded them to be baptized in the name of the Lord.

ARRANGEMENT 30—The Light of the Spirit.

The North aisle of the Church has two light and wide windows of the
are used for arrangements depicting the theme of Whitsuntide. Red is th
two arrange

ARRANGEMENT 31—The Unity of the Spirit.

…d design. These and the Early Norman Cable Font East of the windows
…colour for this Feast of the Holy Spirit. This colour predominates in the
…ated above.

ARRANGEMENT 32—The Gifts of the Spirit.

This Eleventh Century Font cut from one piece of stone, and modelled
after the shape of a Norman water butt—with its stakes at the bottom and
cables at the top, lends great beauty to the delicate circular flower arrangement
done in pink and light red with silver and light green foliage—expresses the
Gifts of the Spirit. It is convenient also that the Sanctification Pillar of the
Holy Trinity theme rises behind the font. The base of the pillar can just be
seen, but the whole pillar is illustrated opposite p.60 (Arrangement 35).
The Parish Register of Baptisms dates back to 1570.

VIII. WHITSUNTIDE—RENEWAL

1. THE LIGHT OF THE SPIRIT.   2. THE UNITY OF THE SPIRIT.

3. THE GIFTS OF THE SPIRIT.

Readings from the Epistles and Gospels for Whitsuntide

A CONDITIONAL PROMISE

. . . 'If you love me you will obey my commands; and I
will ask the Father, and he will give you another to be your
Advocate, who will be with you for ever—the Spirit of truth
. . . then you will know that I am in my Father, and you in me
and I in you . . . but your Advocate, the Holy Spirit whom the
Father will send in my name, will teach you everything, and will
call to mind all that I have told you. . . . Peace is my parting
gift to you, my own peace, such as the world cannot give. Set
your troubled hearts at rest, and banish your fears . . . the world
must be shown that I love the Father, and do exactly as he
commands; so up, let us go forward!' (Gospel, Whit Sunday).

ACTIVELY FULFILLED

. . . they were all together in one place, when suddenly
there came from the sky a noise like that of a strong driving
wind, which filled the whole house where they were sitting.
And there appeared to them tongues like flames of fire, dispersed
among them and resting on each one. And they were all filled
with the Holy Spirit and began to talk in other tongues, as the
Spirit gave them power of utterance . . . (Epistle, Whit Sunday).

. . . on the Gentiles also was poured out the gift of the
Holy Spirit . . . (Epistle, Monday in Whitsun Week) . . . the
honest man comes to the light so that it may be clearly seen
that God is in all he does (Gospel, Monday in Whitsun Week).

THE COLLECT FOR WHIT SUNDAY

God, who as at this time didst teach the hearts of thy faithful people, by the sending to them the light of thy Holy Spirit; Grant us by the same Spirit to have a right judgement in all things, and evermore to rejoice in his holy comfort; through the merits of Jesus Christ our Saviour, who liveth and reigneth with thee, in the unity of the same Spirit, one God, world without end. Amen.

Meditation on the Epistles and Gospels for Whitsuntide

With a strong driving wind the Holy Spirit came to breathe new life into a body of men and women who had been the followers of Jesus, and they were born as a corporate body, the Church, to represent Christ's Body on earth. We keep a remembrance of this great light of the Holy Spirit, bearing Unity and an abundance of Spiritual Gifts, at Whitsuntide. But it must be more than a remembrance of the past. We keep it as a time of renewal. The Spirit of Truth is ours. We have him in our midst in the Church. But too often in recent years we have, by corporate self criticism of a destructive nature and by doubts, marred our corporate witness under the Holy Spirit. So that the unbeliever has no clear faith presented to him. We need men and women to stand up with renewed faith and say: 'I believe'. We need renewed constancy of faith for each Truth of the Church's Year. And we need it every year and most of all during the season of re-birth and renewal at Whitsuntide.

The Spirit of Truth as found in the One, Holy Catholic, Apostolic Church is the Light and Unity in the world which draws men and women to Jesus as Lord of their lives. The application of this faith to our own lives is the only way to convince the unbeliever. God must be seen to be in all our actions.

Peter commanded them to be baptised
in the Name of the Lord

Now that Jesus has ascended His lordship is communicated to the world through His Apostles. They have already been commissioned by Him:

"As the Father sent me, so I send you . . . " (Gospel, Easter I).

And given the power to forgive sins in His Name:

" . . . He then breathed on them, saying, 'Receive the Holy Spirit! If you forgive any man's sins, they stand forgiven; if you pronounce them unforgiven, unforgiven they remain.'" (Gospel, Easter I).

Now, at Pentecost His promise of a Comforter coming to empower them is fulfilled. "If I go, I will send him to you." (John xvi.7b). And from that day the Apostles became the representative Body of Jesus on earth.

And there has grown a corporate body which has extended the knowledge of Jesus as Lord to every corner of the earth. In the power of the Holy Spirit received at Pentecost the Apostles carried out Jesus' commission and baptised in His Name all those who were prepared to accept His lordship. Thus enlarging the corporate body which St. Paul wrote about as the Body of Christ or the Church.

As Christians, mostly by Infant Baptism and Confirmation, we have at some time accepted that 'Jesus is Lord', and by this acceptance we committed ourselves to a common way of life. That is the common life of the Body of Christ, which in everything accepts the lordship of Jesus. And here 'common life' means living and working together in a vast undertaking in the Name of Jesus to extend His lordship to all.

We may depend on it that Jesus is the Word, and that the Holy Spirit in the Church will guide us into all truth concerning Him. But equally Jesus must depend upon us for 'action' now that He has ascended. And because He is Lord of all, the 'action' of His Church must be seen to be 'common action'. Too often individual Christians, and small or large Christian communities act in isolation. Localised action is an essential part of the work of the Church. But it cannot of itself and by itself display the full "Common Life" which proclaims that Jesus is Lord of All.

But the COMMON LIFE OF THE BODY OF CHRIST in action and in our generation is a subject beyond the size of this book. Another book may one day shout this cause in all its many aspects and modern needs. At present our concern is to establish that the Scriptures proclaim that 'Jesus is Lord' in each and every one of the Seasons of the Church's Year.

Demonstrated in our three floral arrangements for Whitsuntide are the Light of the Spirit, the Unity of the Spirit, and the Gifts of the Spirit. We have already thought about the Holy Spirit enlightening our minds in all things concerning the lordship of Jesus, and of the indwelling power by which we are assisted to a common life under the same Lord. The Gifts of the Spirit are bestowed upon the believer to assist him in his work of revealing the light which he has received, in his growth towards perfect obedience under Jesus as Lord, and in his living of a common life with all believers in the Church for the sake of all men.

Just as Jesus gathered together a small band of followers during His earthly ministry for the sake of all men; so it must be that the Church's gatherings of groups of believers must not create an exclusive society: it must always be outward looking and for the sake of all men.

This does not mean that the Church should compromise the perfect standard of living set by Jesus, for the sake of men, or the Spirit of Truth as received in the One, Holy Catholic, Apostolic Church. Any lowering of standards as to morals or as to faith must inevitably lead to a lesser witness of Jesus as Lord.

Often we are tempted to diminish the standards of the Gospel or remove essential matters of faith in the hope of attracting the unbeliever to the Church. But this cannot be done in the Name of Jesus. Though He was the Son of God, He died for our sakes rather than lower His standards, or alter His faith in the fact that He was the Resurrection and the Life, without question and without compromise.

Chapter IX

•

TRINITY

THREE IN ONE, AND ONE IN THREE

•

READINGS FROM SOME OF THE TRINITYTIDE EPISTLES

MEDITATION ON SOME OF THE TRINITYTIDE EPISTLES

•

ARRANGEMENTS 33, 34 and 35

33 Creation
34 Redemption
35 Sanctification

•

READING FROM THE EPISTLE FOR TRINITY SUNDAY

MEDITATION ON THE EPISTLE FOR TRINITY SUNDAY

•

ARRANGEMENTS 36, 37, 38 and 39

36 Divine Majesty and Glory
37 A Rainbow round about the Throne
38 Crowns of Gold
39 A Jasper and Cornelian

•

THE LORD OUR RIGHTEOUSNESS

ARRANGEMENT 37—A Rainbow round about the Throne
in sight like unto an Emerald.

This theme from the Revelation of St. John the Divine is shown on the altar in the Children's Chapel and in the East window. The window displays the rainbow, with the boy-bishop holding the lamb in the centre of the arrangement. The two vases on the altar hold dark green foliage only, to depict the sight of an emerald.

IX. TRINITY—THREE IN ONE, AND ONE IN THREE

1. THE FATHER—CREATION.   2. THE SON—REDEMPTION.
3. THE HOLY SPIRIT—SANCTIFICATION

Readings from some of the Trinitytide Epistles

GOD IS RIGHTEOUS AND HOLY

' . . . Holy, holy, holy is God the sovereign Lord of all, who was, and is, and is to come!' . . . 'Thou art worthy, O Lord our God, to receive glory and honour and power, because thou didst create all things; by thy will they were created, and have their being!' . . . (Epistle, Trinity Sunday) . . . and this is his Name whereby he shall be called, THE LORD OUR RIGHTEOUS-NESS . . . (Epistle, Trinity XXV).

AND THERE ARE THREE PERSONS IN ONE GOD

. . . No one can say, 'Jesus is Lord!' except under the influence of the Holy Spirit. There are varieties of gifts, but the same Spirit. There are varieties of service, but the same Lord. There are many forms of work, but all of them, in all men, are the work of the same God . . . (Epistle, Trinity X).

GOD HAS CHILDREN

. . . All who are moved by the Spirit of God are sons of God. The Spirit you have received is not the spirit of slavery leading you back into a life of fear, but the Spirit that makes us sons, enabling us to cry 'Abba! Father!' In that cry the Spirit of God joins with our spirit in testifying that we are God's children . . . we are God's heirs and Christ's fellow-heirs, if we share his sufferings now in order to share his splendour hereafter (Epistle, Trinity VIII).

TO WHOM HE IS FAITHFUL

. . . God keeps faith, and he will not allow you to be tested above your powers, but when the test comes he will at the same time provide a way out, by enabling you to sustain it (Epistle, Trinity IX).

AND GOD IS LOVE

. . . let us love one another, because love is from God. Everyone that loves is a child of God and knows God . . . For God is love; and his love was disclosed to us in this, that he sent his only Son into the world to bring us life . . . Though God has never been seen by any man, God himself dwells in us if we love one another; his love is brought to perfection in us (Epistle, Trinity I).

The Collect for Trinity VII

Lord of all power and might, who art the author and giver of all good things; Graft in our hearts the love of thy Name, increase in us true religion, nourish us with all goodness, and of thy great mercy keep us in the same; through Jesus Christ our Lord. Amen.

The Collect for Trinity XI

O God, who declarest thy almighty power most chiefly in shewing mercy and pity; Mercifully grant unto us such a measure of thy grace, that we, running the way of thy commandments, may obtain thy gracious promises, and be made partakers of thy heavenly treasure; through Jesus Christ our Lord. Amen.

The Collect for the Sunday Next Before Advent

Stir up, we beseech thee, O Lord, the wills of thy faithful people; that they, plenteously bringing forth the fruit of good works, may of thee be plenteously rewarded; through Jesus Christ our Lord. Amen.

Meditation on Some of the Trinitytide Epistles

Each of us will have our own deep meditations on the Mystery of the Holy Trinity. But out of them we must all come to the same conclusion as believers, and that is: that God, the Father and Creator is Love; that God, the Son and Redeemer is Love; and that God, the Holy Spirit and Sanctifier is Love.

And there is no way in which we, as the children of God by faith and grace, can reveal him to our neighbour except by loving him as God's creation, for whom Jesus died, and with whom we are sanctified by the Holy Spirit.

The Lord our Righteousness

We have studied the confession of the lordship of Jesus in relation to ourselves through all the Seasons of the Church's Year except Trinitytide. In the Season of Trinity, which extends over half the year, we find practical evidence in the Epistles and Gospels for all that we claim for Jesus. Any summary of all this evidence will bring us to consider the authority of His lordship. Righteousness is His authority as Lord. The righteousness of God is His, and in Himself He is the righteousness of man. He is 'The Lord our Righteousness'. His was a righteousness measured by love. His first commandment for living is 'Love God', and His second 'Love they neighbour as thyself'. And motive is the test of every action, if it is to be judged righteous in His Name and for His sake. No authority is true or lasting which rests simply upon a superimposed title, rank, or position of power over others. But authority is valid and permanent in so far as the lordship of the person in authority is conducted in righteousness to God and man. In this sense we can confess without reservation that 'Jesus is Lord'.

But in regard to righteousness there is another sense in which his lordship is to be seen and known. We say so often: "The grace of our Lord Jesus Christ . . . " But how often do we relate His grace to His lordship? He is our Righteousness, and under such a lordship as his our righteousness can only grow through love and faith.

A believer seeks a right relationship with God and finds it in the forgiveness of sins; and he seeks to perfect it in acts of love as a thanksgiving for the forgiveness of his sins.

We began the Church's Year with the subject of mission. We now see mission as a demonstration of the Righteousness of Jesus in our teaching and in our living, which is achieved by faith in the lordship of Jesus over our teaching and our living.

But all this is vanity unless we have in our heart the faith that God raised Jesus from the dead. This faith within the personal life of the believer gives power to his mission for Christ.

Whatever words are spoken or written, it is the evidence of the Risen life of Jesus, working in and through the lives of those who claim Him to be Lord, which challenges the un-believer. And this is not only a matter of individual witness, it is also the concern of the corporate witness of the Church.

Those who cannot believe in their heart that God raised Jesus from the dead are dishonest to God if they claim to hold any position of authority in the Church, however exalted or humble that position may be. The lordship of Jesus and the authority He has delegated to the Church, His Body, in the power of the Holy Spirit must rest on the faith that God raised Him from the dead.

Without this faith a man, whatever his status in the Church, speaks on his own authority. And when he speaks he is dishonest unless he makes this fact plain to the public.

There are many today within the Church who are daubing the true Faith of the Church with untempered mortar.

But let them hear what the prophet Ezekiel has written in the Name of the Lord:

"Thus saith the Lord God; Woe unto the foolish prophets, that follow their own spirit, and have seen nothing . . . Ye have not gone into the gaps, neither made up the hedge of the house of Israel to stand in the battle in the day of the Lord. . . . Have ye not seen a vain vision, and have ye not spoken a lying divination, whereas ye say. The Lord saith it; albeit I have not spoken? . . . they shall not be in the council of my people."(Ezekiel xiii.3, 5, 7 & 8. AV).

ARRANGEMENT
36
Divine Majesty and
Glory
White flowers in
threefold design are
seen with a back-
ground of dark,
light, and flecked
green foliage for
the pillar themes of
creation, redemp-
tion and sanctifica-
tion.

Below: ARRANGEMENT 38—Crowns of Gold
This is another floral representation of St. John's vision, showing those clothed
in white raiment with crowns of gold upon their heads.

THE BLESSED and HOLY TRINITY

The body of this Church has two pillars which support the roof and open the way from the Nave to the North side aisle. These are chosen for foliage arrangements depicting—Creation, in dark green and—Redemption, in light green. A third and smaller pillar opening the way to the transept is used to depict—Sanctification, in flecked green and yellow foliage. Throughout the Church the mystery of the Trinity has been shown with foliage arrangements darkest at the Creation pillar, spreading to North, South, and West getting lighter in green, and lightest through the chancel and sanctuary to the altar at the East end.

(left)
ARRANGEMENT 33—Creation
Dark green foliage.

(left)
ARRANGEMENT 35—Sanctification
Flecked green foliage.

(below)
ARRANGEMENT 34—Redemption
Light green foliage.

ARRANGEMENT 39
A Jasper and Cornelian.
(see description of these stones mentioned by St. John under Briefing No. 1, p.71).

TRINITY—THREE IN ONE, AND ONE IN THREE

  4. DIVINE MAJESTY AND GLORY.

  5. ROUND THE THRONE WAS A RAINBOW.

  6. CROWNS OF GOLD.

  7. THE GLEAM OF JASPER AND CORNELIAN.

Reading from the Epistle for Trinity Sunday

ST. JOHN'S VISION OF THE THRONE IN HEAVEN

After this I looked, and there before my eyes was a door opened in heaven; and the voice that I had first heard speaking to me like a trumpet said, 'Come up here and I will show you what must happen hereafter'. At once I was caught up by the Spirit. There in heaven stood a throne, and on the throne sat one whose appearance was like the gleam of jasper and cornelian; and round the throne was a rainbow, bright as an emerald. In a circle about this throne were twenty-four other thrones, and on them sat twenty-four elders, robed in white and wearing crowns of gold . . . the twenty-four elders fall down before the One who sits on the throne and worship him who lives for ever and ever; and as they lay their crowns before the throne they cry: "Thou art worthy, O Lord our God, to receive glory and honour and power, because thou didst create all things; by thy will they were created, and have their being!" (Epistle, Trinity Sunday).

THE COLLECT FOR TRINITY SUNDAY

Almighty and everlasting God, who hast given unto us thy servants grace by the confession of a true faith to acknowledge the glory of the eternal Trinity, and in the power of the Divine Majesty to worship the Unity; We beseech thee, that thou wouldest keep us stedfast in this faith, and evermore defend us from all adversities, who livest and reignest, one God, world without end. Amen.

Meditation on the Epistle for Trinity Sunday

THE INTERPRETATION OF VISIONS

No man can properly interpret another man's vision. For as everyone sees a different rainbow, so each man's vision is his own and he alone can offer an interpretation of what it means to him. We can, however, enter the beauty of St. John's description and thoughts and find some message for ourselves. If this is so, it is necessary to use the first person singular and tell what I see in this vision of the throne of God and the people and things around the throne and all other symbolic descriptions. In all the stones named in this Epistle there is green, and green is the liturgical colour for the season of Trinity. This is appropriate since in the earth there is green everywhere. The trees and the earth are clothed by God in an infinite variety of hues of green, and the flowers are surrounded, protected, and fed by their green clothing. Also in the earth God's hand is everywhere creating, redeeming, and sanctifying. For this reason the floral decorators of this Church have tried, each in their own vision of God's loving purpose for man, season by season in the Church's Year, to show in beauty some symbol of the Truth. With green foliage, like the gleam of St. John's jasper and cornelian, they have tried to express in a vision the Mystery of the Holy and Blessed Trinity on the pillars of the Church. At the same time they have allowed the hues of foliage, their symbol of Mystery, to spread through all the arrangements, giving a sense of the presence of God, Father, Son and Spirit in every season of the year.

Have you your own vision of the Majesty and Glory of God? If you have, you should not always keep it locked in your heart. Expressing it in your life by word or action may well help others to see that the love of God dwells in you. And in this way you will help each other to know God better.

Chapter X

Some Briefings

for

Flower Festivals

in

Churches

INDEX OF BRIEFINGS

X. SOME BRIEFINGS FOR FLOWER FESTIVALS IN CHURCHES

The first 'briefing' is a copy of the actual suggestions put before the Dorset Floral Decoration Society prior to the Flower Festival which has been the main subject of this book. After general discussion of the plan by the appropriate floral committee, the general direction of the Festival was undertaken by Mrs. Cara Barne (Bere Regis F.D.S.) with the following Societies undertaking to do groups of arrangements according to the Seasons of the Church's Year: Sturminster Newton, Blandford, Bere Regis, Wareham, Wimborne, Dorchester, Dorchester Evening, Marnhull, and Parkstone. Each Society received copies of the 'briefing' on which Mrs. Barne added her own notes concerning technical arrangement details. (These are not included in the copy below, since this book claims no authoritative knowledge concerning the art of flower arranging as such.) The Societies were then left an entirely free hand as to how much or little of the 'briefing' they used to interpret the themes allocated to them. The success and competence of their work can be seen in the book's colour illustrations. But it must be remembered that the total picture of the interpretation of Meditations in Flowers was directed by Mrs. Barne, who inspired a spirit of friendliness and co-operation between all concerned which led to the correlation of diverse gifted personalities into a corporate body working together to present a Christian message through flowers. A spirit of competition aids the advancement of flower arranging as a technique at Flower Shows. But it is important at a Church Flower Festival that this competitive spirit is replaced by a spirit of overall pattern and co-operation between arrangers under a director. "The widow's mite", or the penitent man at prayer saying: "Lord, I am not worthy", might be appropriate parables to guide the arranger's work in a church. There are Nine Seasonal Themes in the first 'briefing'. But using any one as the general title for a Church Flower Festival, it would not be difficult to extend it and build it up into a 'briefing' on that theme alone.

BRIEFING NO. 1. — THE CHURCH'S YEAR.

General Title of the Festival....

MEDITATION IN FLOWERS depicting THE RENEWAL OF FAITH according to the CHURCH'S YEAR.

Nine Main Themes.

1. Saint Andrew   4 arrangements—in the porch.

2. Advent . .   1 arrangement S. wall window (W. of porch).

3. Christmas .   4 arrangements—S. wall window (E. of porch).

4. Epiphany .   2 arrangements—inside the porch door.

5. Lent . . .   6 arrangements—from vestry screen to prayer stall.

6. Easter . .   8 arrangements—in the chancel and sanctuary.

7. Ascension .   4 arrangements—W. end font and W. window.

8. Whitsuntide   3 arrangements—N. wall windows and Norman font.

9. Trinity . .   7 arrangements—3 pillars and the N. chapel.

I.   **SAINT ANDREW—Mission.** Red is the liturgical colour for Saint Andrew. Could this colour predominate in these arrangements? Suggest the 4 positions in the porch—2 reaching to the church door and 2 out into the world—to express missionary activity.

     4 arrangements in positions 1, 2, 3, 4.

Meditation: "How shall they hear without a preacher?" and "All day long I have stretched forth my hands unto a disobedient and recalcitrant people".

II. **ADVENT—Darkness to Light.** Violet and blue are the liturgical colours for Advent.

1 arrangement in position 5.

Could the arrangement be positioned in the S. wall window (W. of the porch)?

Meditation: Collect . . . . "that we may cast off the works of darkness, and put upon us the armour of light." See also Epistle for Advent Sunday.

III. **CHRISTMAS—Incarnation—**

4 arrangements numbered 6—9.

1. Christmas Day. The Nativity. S. wall window (E. of porch). White and gold are the liturgical colours for Christmas. Could one or two figures from the Crib be used?

Position 6.

Meditation: "Born of a pure Virgin", the Collect and Gospel for Christmas Day—especially—" In Him was life, and the life was the light of men."

2. Saint Stephen. Martyrdom. In front of the pulpit.

Position 7.

Deep red is liturgical colour for martyrs.

Meditation: The Collect and Epistle for St. Stephen's Day—specially "looking up stedfastly into heaven".

3. Holy Innocents Day: Innocence. On the pulpit,

Position 9.

close to the wall. Red is the liturgical colour, suggest light red or pink or both.

Meditation: The Collect for Holy Innocents Day.

4. Saint John's Day. Truth. In front of the lectern.

Position 8.

White is the liturgical colour.

Meditation: "The Light of thy truth". The Collect for St. John's Day.

IV.   **EPIPHANY—Manifestation—**
> 2 arrangements numbered 10 and 11.

1. The Three Kings. Gifts. Suggest a small table inside the S. door. Could the figures of the Three Kings from the Crib be used? And could gold, frankincence and myrrh be depicted? White is the liturgical colour for Epiphany.

Position 10.

Meditation: The Gospel for the Epiphany. Specially: "They presented unto him gifts; gold, frankincence and myrrh."

2. The Star. Guidance. Could the star arrangement be situated on the S. wall? Thus leading the eye from the 'Gifts' arrangement to the Christmas window.

Position 11.

Meditation: The Collect and Gospel for the Epiphany. Specially: "When they saw the star, they rejoiced with exceeding great joy." and "O God, who by the leading of a star didst manifest thy only-begotten Son to the Gentiles."

V.   **LENT—Fasting and Suffering—**
> 6 arrangements numbered 12—17.

1. Lent i-iv. Penitence. Blue or violet are the liturgical colours for Lent. Suggest the first panel (L to R) of the vestry screen.

Position 12.

Meditation: Gospel for Ash Wednesday. Specially: "Where your treasure is, there shall your heart be also".

2. Passion Sunday. Passion. Suggest the second panel of the vestry screen. Liturgical colour as per (1), but suggest introduction of blood red to depict the Passion.

Position 13.

Meditation: The Epistle for Lent V. Specially: "How much more shall the blood of Christ . . . . purge your conscience from dead works to serve the living God".

3. Palm Sunday. Triumph.

Position 14.

The third panel of the vestry screen. The liturgical colour as in (1) and (2), but would suggest a colour brighter than violet is introduced to express—triumph. Two or three palms of the right size can be provided if required.

Meditation: The Epistle for Palm Sunday. Specially: "That at the name of Jesus every knee should bow . . ."

4. Maundy Thursday. Communion.

Position 15.

The fourth panel of the vestry screen. Liturgical colour as in (1), (2) and (3), but would suggest that wine colour predominates. Chalice and paten can be lent for use with the arrangement if required.

Meditation: Collect for the Institution of the Blessed Sacrament. Specially "Who in a wonderful sacrament has left us a memorial of his passion . . ."

5. Good Friday. Sacrifice.

Positions 16 and 17.

Suggest the shelf with the crucifix under the picture of the Madonna and Child. Also the N. prayer stall pew end and chancel step. Liturgical colour as before but suggest the use of deep red.

Meditation: The First Collect and the Gospel for Good Friday. Specially: "And to suffer death upon the cross . . ." and "They shall look on him whom they pierced".

VI. EASTER—Resurrection—

8 arrangements numbered 18—25.

1. The Empty Tomb. Life through death.

Position 18.

The liturgical colour for the whole season of Easter should be predominantly white. Could the

Elizabethan tomb be used for this position? Also suggest use of wrapped linen?

Meditation: Easter Anthem. Specially: "Christ is risen from the dead . . . " and the Gospel for Easter Day: "And seeth the linen clothes lie . . . "

2. The Altar. The Gate of Everlasting Life. Altar vases

Positions 19 and 20.

and pedestals to R. and L. of altar.

Meditation: Easter Collect: "Jesus Christ hath overcome death and opened unto us the gate of everlasting life". and the Epistle for Easter Day: "If ye then be risen with Christ seek those things which are above . . . "

3. Easter i.—Pureness of Living. Suggest the Nativity

Position 21.

window to the R. of the altar in the S. wall.

Meditation: Collect for Easter I. Specially: "That we may also serve thee in pureness of living and truth".

4. Easter ii.—Exemplary Living. Suggest the Good

Position 22.

Shepherd window second to R. in S. wall.

Meditation: Collect for Easter II. Specially: "Also an exsample of godly life . . . "

5. Easter iii.—Joy of Living. Suggest the three L. panels

Position 23.

of the vestry screen behind the choir stalls. They are situated next to the Good Friday arrangement (17). Could this and (6) and (7) following show a progression from sorrow to joy, using the liturgical colour for penitence (violet or blue) through martyrdom (deep red) and the Holy Spirit (light red) for the Glory of Living, and all three for the Victory of Living?

Meditation: Gospel for Easter III. " . . . your sorrow shall be turned into joy . . . "

6. Easter iv.—Glory of Living. Suggest the three R.
Position 24. panels of the same screen. Colours as suggested above in (5).

Meditation: Collect, Epistle and Gospel for Easter IV. Specially: " . . . He shall glorify me: for he shall receive of mine, and shall show it unto you".

7. Easter v.—Victory of Living. Suggest the archway above the panels for Joy of
Position 25. Living and Glory of Living. Colours as suggested in (5) above.

Meditation: Gospel for Easter V. Specially: " . . . but be of good cheer, I have overcome the world".

VII. **ASCENSIONTIDE—Ascension.—**
4 arrangements numbered 26—29.

1. Ascension Day—Love ascending into the heavens.
Suggest W. font and W. window
Positions 26-28 under tower. Three arrange-ments (i) base of font; (ii) on font cover; (iii) in window, giving upward steps effect.

Meditation: Collect for Ascension Day. Specially: " . . . so we may also in heart and mind thither ascend, and with him continually dwell.

2. Sunday after Ascension.—Love ascending and de-scending. Suggest high window
Position 29. over W. side door. Love lifted up and reaching down to cover the sins of man.

Meditation: Epistle for Ascension I. Specially: " . . . for charity shall cover the multitude of sins . . . "

VIII. **WHITSUNTIDE—Renewal.—**
3 arrangements numbered 30—32.

1. The Light of the Spirit. The liturgical colour for

Position 30.　　　　　Whitsun is red. Suggest the L. window of the N. wall.

Meditation: Collect for Whit Sunday. Specially: " . . . by the sending to them the Light of thy Holy Spirit . . . "

2. The Unity of the Spirit. Suggest the R. window of the N. wall. This seen from the

Position 31.　　　　　porch door has the advantage of standing between the main pillars and the side chapel pillar (all represent—the Trinity).

Meditation: Collect for Whit Sunday. Specially: " . . . in the unity of the same Spirit . . . "

3. The Gifts of the Spirit. Suggest the Norman font.
　　　Position 32.

Meditation: Epistle for Whit Sunday. Specially: "and there appeared unto them cloven tongues, like as of fire . . . etc. . . . "

IX.　　**TRINITY—Three in One and One in Three.—**
　　　　　7 arrangements numbered 33—39.
　　　　　Liturgical colour green.

1. The Father.—Creation. Suggest predominance of dark green on the main W. pillar.

2. The Son.—Redemption. Suggest predominance of light green in the main E. pillar.

3. The Holy Spirit.—Sanctification. Suggest predominance of green flecked with white, yellow or red on pillar to side chapel

4. Divine Majesty and Glory. Suggest all three greens as background to an abundance of bright colours. L. of vestry door.

Meditation: The Collect and Epistle for Trinity Sunday: Specially: " . . . to acknowledge the glory of the Eternal Trinity . . . " and "Thou art worthy, O Lord to receive glory, and honour, and power . . . "

5. A rainbow round the throne. Suggest green on side chapel altar for the emerald, and rainbow of bright colours above in window.
Position 37.

Meditation: Epistle for Trinity Sunday. Specially: " . . . and there was a rainbow round about the throne, in sight like unto an emerald".

6. Crowns of Gold. Suggest N. window of side chapel.
Position 38.

Meditation: Epistle for Trinity Sunday. Specially: " . . . clothed in white raiment; and they had on their heads crowns of gold . . . "

7. Jasper and cornelian stones. Suggest W. window of side chapel.
Position 39.

Meditation: Epistle for Trinity Sunday. Specially: " . . . and he that sat was to look upon like a jasper and cornelian stone . . . "

N.B. Jasper stone=an impure variety of quartz, of many colours and shades, or a greenish marble with small red spots. Cornelian=a precious stone. A variety of agate or onyx (quartz resembling agate with varying coloured layers) composed of white chalcedony alternating with layers of sard.

General remarks: It is only suggested that the liturgical colours are used where possible in any theme, and they could be the dominant colour or just the background colour.

It is thought that it might be interesting and suggestive of the beauty of dark and light shades (and darkness to light in Christian teaching) if this could be brought out by green backgrounds to arrangements being darkest at the Creation pillar, spreading N.S. and W, getting lighter in green, and lightest through the sanctuary to the altar in the E. The nine main themes suggest that the arrangers might work together as individuals, pairs, or teams according to the number of arrangements required in each theme.

BRIEFING No. 2.—THE SERMON ON THE MOUNT

General Title of the Festival . . .

BEATITUDES AND FLOWERS depicting the MORAL TEACHING OF JESUS according to the SERMON ON THE MOUNT.

Ten Main Themes

1. The Poor.	6. The Pure.
2. The Sorrowful.	7. The Peacemakers.
3. The Gentle.	8. The Persecuted.
4. The Righteous.	9. The Salt of the Earth.
5. The Merciful.	10. The Light of the World.

The location for each theme will depend upon the particular Church which is to be decorated. And the number of arrangements used to depict each theme will depend upon the ideas stimulated by the following texts or other related Scriptural teaching.

This is a difficult 'briefing' to execute in flowers. But a short companion brochure for meditation would assist the interpretation of the themes.

1. **The Poor.** One or more arrangements to interpret the following:

    (a) "How blest are those who know that they are poor; the kingdom of Heaven is theirs" (Matt.v.3).

    (b) " . . . poor ourselves, we bring wealth to many . . . " (II Cor.vi.10).

    (c) " . . . penniless, we own the world . . . " (ditto).

    (d) (Jesus Christ) " . . . was rich, yet for your sake he became poor, so that through his poverty you might become rich" (II Cor.viii.9).

    Suggest the use of a crucifix with the floral arrangement.

    (e) "You say, 'How rich I am! And how well I have done! I have everything I want in the world. In fact, though you do not know it, you are the most pitiful wretch, poor, blind, and naked. So I advise you to buy from me gold refined in the fire, to make you truly rich, and white clothes to put on to hide the shame of your nakedness, and ointment for your eyes so that you may see" (Rev.iii.17—18).

2. The Sorrowful. One or more arrangements to interpret the following:

(a) "How blest are the sorrowful; they shall find consolation" (Matt. v.4).

(b) "In our sorrows we have always cause for joy" (II Cor.vi.10).

3. The Gentle. One or more arrangements to interpret the following:

(a) "How blest are those of a gentle spirit; they shall have the earth for their possession" (Matt.v.5).

(b) "Come to me, all whose work is hard, whose load is heavy; and I will give you relief. Bend your necks to my yoke, and learn from me, for I am gentle and humble-hearted; and your souls will find relief. For my yoke is good to bear, my load is light" (Matt.xi.28—30).

(c) "Your beauty should reside, not in outward adornment—the braiding of the hair, or jewellery, or dress—but in the inmost centre of your being, with this imperishable ornament, a gentle, quiet spirit, which is of high value in the sight of God" (I Pet.iii.3—4).

4. The Righteous. One or more arrangements to interpret the following:

(a) "How blest are those who hunger and thirst to see right prevail; they shall be satisfied" (Matt.v.6).

(b) " . . . put yourselves at the disposal of God, as dead men raised to life; yield your bodies to him as implements for doing right" (Rom. vi.13b).

(c) . . . 'the wedding-day of the Lamb has come! His bride has made herself ready, and for her dress she has been given fine linen, clean and shining.' (Now the fine linen signifies the righteous deeds of God's people.)" (Rev.xix.7b—8).

5. The Merciful. One or more arrangements to interpret the following:

(a) "How blest are those who show mercy; mercy shall be shown to them" (Matt.v.7).

If there is a stained glass window of the Good Samaritan. This would be a good position for the arrangement:—

6. The Pure. One or more arrangements to interpret the following:

> (a) "How blest are those whose hearts are pure; they shall see God" (Matt.v.8).
>
> (b) "To the pure all things are pure; but nothing is pure to the tainted minds of disbelievers, tainted alike in reason and conscience" (Titus.i.15).
>
> (c) "Then he showed me the river of the water of life, sparkling like crystal . . . " (Rev.xxii.1).

7. The Peacemakers. One or more arrangements to interpret the following:

> (a) "How blest are the peacemakers; God shall call them his sons" (Matt.v.9).
>
> (b) "Let us then pursue the things that make for peace and build up the common life" (Rom.xiv.19).

8. The Persecuted. One or more arrangements to interpret the following:

> "How blest are those who have suffered persecution for the cause of right; the kingdom of Heaven is theirs" (Matt.v.10).

This theme could be taken with (4) above. See also references to St. Stephen on pp.25 & 26.

9. The Salt of the Earth. Probably this theme ought to be depicted together with (10) below. It should interpret the following:

> "You are salt to the world . . . " (Matt.v.13).

10. The Light of the World.

> "You are the light of all the world . . . When a lamp is lit, it is not put under the meal-tub, but on the lamp-stand, where it gives light to everyone in the house" (Matt.v.14—15).

See also references to Light and Darkness under Advent p.17f. Scripture passages concerning this theme are so numerous and suggestive of interpretation by floral arrangements that it would be an easy matter to devise a 'briefing' with it as the General Title of a Festival.

BRIEFING No. 3.—A PATRONAL FESTIVAL

It should not be difficult to devise a 'briefing' for the commemoration of the Patron Saint of any Church in terms of a Flower Festival. As an example, here is a 'briefing' for St. Mary the Virgin.

General Title of the Festival . . .

PATRONAL FESTIVAL IN FLOWERS depicting THE LIFE OF THE BLESSED VIRGIN MARY.

Ten Main Themes

1. The Nativity of the Virgin Mary.
2. The Visitation.
3. The Annunciation.
4. The Conception.
5. The Birth of Jesus.
6. The Purification.
7. The Epiphany.
8. The Passover at Jerusalem.
9. The Marriage at Cana.
10. The Crucifixion.

BRIEFING No. 4.—A MESSAGE TO THE CHURCHES

General Title of the Festival . . .

REVELATION IN FLOWERS depicting a MESSAGE FROM CHRIST TO THE CHURCHES according to SAINT JOHN THE DIVINE.

This is another 'briefing' difficult to execute, but by no means impossible. It is probable that very skilled arrangers would be required to obtain the right effects. Also each arranger would need to have a picture of the 'whole' to get the right emphasis in a particular arrangement. To do this the whole of Chapters 1—3 of the Revelation of St. John should be read and studied.

For preference a cathedral or large parish church would be necessary as a location for the Festival.

Fifteen Main Themes

1. **The Alpha and Omega.** Suggest this arrangement should be the dominant feature of the Festival. That it should be large and perhaps horseshoe-shaped on either side and under the feet of a figure of Christ in Glory, or Christ the King, as is found in some churches.

> " . . . when I turned I saw seven standing lamps of gold, and among the lamps one like a son of man, robed down to his feet, with a golden girdle round his breast. The hair of his head was white as snow-white wool, and his eyes flamed like fire; his feet gleamed like burnished brass refined in a furnace, and his voice was like the sound of rushing waters. In his right hand he held seven stars, and out of his mouth came a sharp two-edged sword; and his face shone like the sun in full strength" (Rev.i.12—16).

Suggest that each of the seven stars on the right hand be in different colours, in all giving a rainbow colour effect, and that these colours are repeated severally in the seven star arrangements representing the angels of the seven churches (see 9—15 below).

2. **The Golden Lamp of Ephesus.** Suggest gold should be the dominant colour in this and each of the other arrangements representing the churches. And that there should be a secondary colour in each according to the message to each church. For Ephesus it might well be strong violet or blue for fortitude and repentance. Also vine leaves and grapes (read Rev.ii.1—7).

3. **The Golden Lamp of Smyrna.** Gold dominant (possibly crown shaped). Secondary, white for Resurrection and red for persecution (read Rev.ii.8—11).

4. **The Golden Lamp of Pergamum.** Gold dominant (possibly in the shape of a two-edged sword and situated near the lectern). Secondary, as near black as possible (dark purple tulips) to represent Satan and white, for the white stone traditionally given to express hospitality. This white could be garland shaped, which also expresses welcome or hospitality (read Rev.ii.12—17).

5. **The Golden Lamp of Thyatira.** Gold dominant (possibly yellow and orange to express fire and burnished brass). Secondary, multicoloured to represent Jezebel. If a colour can be devised to express 'authority' this might also be used (read Rev.ii.18—end).

6. **The Golden Lamp of Sardis.** Gold dominant (possibly gold centre of a seven-pointed star, each point a colour to conform with the colours of the seven stars (9—15)). Secondary white in the shape of robes (read Rev.iii.1—6).

7. **The Golden Lamp of Philadelphia.** Gold dominant (possibly key-shaped?) Secondary, rust-brown or amber to express a door (possibly the shape of a pillar, or on a pillar?) (read Rev.iii.7—13).

8. **The Golden Lamp of Laodicea.** Gold dominant (possibly with dark green to express 'creation'). Secondary, red, white and cream for fire, clothes, and ointment. (If there is

a stained glass window expressing 'I stand knocking at the door'—this might be the location) (read Rev.iii.14—end).

The location order of these could be altered to suit colour matching.

> "Here is the secret meaning of the seven stars which you saw in my right hand, and of the seven lamps of gold: the seven stars are the angels of the seven churches, and the seven lamps are the seven churches" (Rev.i.20).

Since the stars are to the right of the central figure, it would be convenient if the seven golden lamp arrangements are placed on the left of the central figure and opposite the appropriate star arrangement.

9. **The Star Angel of Ephesus.** Suggest colours as for (2) above, excluding gold.

10. **The Star Angel of Smyrna.** Suggest colours as for (3) above, excluding gold.

11. **The Star Angel of Pergamum.** Colours as for (4) above, excluding gold.

12. **The Star Angel of Thyatira.** Colours as for (5) above, excluding gold.

13. **The Star Angel of Sardis.** Colours as for (6) above, excluding gold.

14. **The Star Angel of Philadelphia.** Colours as for (7) above, excluding gold.

15. **The Star Angel of Laodicea.** Colours as for (8) above, excluding gold.

In place of the gold each arrangement representing angels could have silver foliage.